KEEPING AMERICA
UNINFORMED

KEEPING AMERICA
UNINFORMED

Government Secrecy in the 1980's

Donna A. Demac

Preface by Ben H. Bagdikian

The Pilgrim Press
New York

Library of Congress Cataloging in Publication Data

Demac, Donna A.
Keeping America uninformed.

Bibliography: p. 169.
Includes index.
1. Executive privilege (Government information)—
United States.   2. Official secrets—United States.
3. Security classification (Government documents)—United States.
4. United States—Politics and government—1981–   .   I. Title.
JK468.S4D45   1984   353.0081'9   84-1013
ISBN 0-8298-0720-9
ISBN 0-8298-0721-7 (pbk)

The Pilgrim Press, 132 West 31 Street, New York, NY 10001

ACKNOWLEDGMENTS

In researching this book, I was assisted by many people, some of whom are mentioned explicitly in the following chapters while others must remain anonymous according to the rules established for congressional staff and federal agency personnel. I wish to acknowledge the generosity of all those whom I interviewed and who forwarded written material to me.

A grant from the Veatch Foundation of the North Shore Unitarian Society paid for printing costs. The Office of Communication of the United Church of Christ supported the project in several ways. I am especially grateful to Beverly J. Chain, director of the Office, for her assistance.

Susan C. Winslow, my editor at Pilgrim Press, deserves my congratulations for her diligence and speed in dealing with the manuscript. Diana Autin, Jan Engsberg, Kathleen Maloy, Tonda Rush, and Katherine Wallman read portions of the initial draft and provided useful comments. Leanne Katz, John Downing, and Arlene Fleming uncovered several pieces of valuable information and analysis. Gene Gaillard, Anthony Santoni, and Dore Steinberg helped gather material and conducted telephone interviews. Melissa Sutherland did an excellent job in typing the manuscript.

I very much appreciate the enduring support and insights of Denison Demac, Ash Corea, Mary Rossman, and Raffie Samach. Philip Mattera has been an unending source of strength and inspiration, equipped with the gentle art of constructive criticism. I must thank him for keen editorial suggestions, indefatigable humor and insight, and other forms of encouragement that shall remain classified.

Despite such high-quality assistance, one may still make mistakes. I accept full responsibility for all the imperfections herein.

CONTENTS

PREFACE
The Calculus of Democracy

A sinister wind is blowing through the American democratic process. We began our society on the principle that government exists legitimately only with the consent of the governed and that consent without significant information is meaningless: the greater the information available to the public, the safer the democracy. But in the last generation, we have reversed that assumption. Thanks to nuclear weapons, the Cold War, and the growing militarization of America, we seem to have accepted the contrary idea that the less the public knows, the greater "the national security."

The Reagan administration has accelerated this reversal of the democratic process. Each year the American public learns less crucial information about its most vital issues: war and peace, military budgets, and the endless struggle between corruption and rectitude in spending public money.

There has been debate about secrecy, as there ought to be. But it has continued so long that much of it reaches the public in exchanges of clichés, of "national security" versus "the public's right to know," or "not aiding the enemy" versus "freedom of information." Those terms have real meaning, but they soon become drained of content. As largely symbolic utterances, they obscure the damning detail. This book ably presents that detail.

Censors seldom need to explain their acts; the rhetoric of superpatriotism diverts attention from the losses that flow from compulsive secrecy. We have been conditioned to accept the alarming scenarios of harm that is presumed to come if a particular piece of information becomes known to the public and therefore to potential adversaries. We are seldom reminded of the disasters that occur regularly throughout history because important information has been kept from the public.

There is almost a formula for the calculus of democracy: a government that presses for zero risk from the consequences of releasing information by that act maximizes damage to the country's political process.

Most governments are tempted to minimize the short-term risks and so are inclined toward secrecy. Heads of state usually prefer to avoid political inconvenience or embarrassment by total disclosure. A president who is able to increase secrecy decreases his accountability to the public.

When secrecy is raised to an almost religious level in the name of "national security," it becomes impossible to know when a withheld fact is, in fact, militarily dangerous or merely politically inconvenient for those in power. But whether kept secret for legitimate military purposes or for self-serving political ones, every significant fact hidden from public view diminishes freedom in society. The society that is given no choices has no real freedom.

The quality of public policy, no less than the quality of science, depends on maximum exposure of data and propositions. The scientific discovery locked instantly in the scientist's safe is the equivalent of a discovery never made. If every scientific insight with potential military application had been perfectly censored, we would all be living in a world that is flat, and we would still be treating diseases by bleeding the sick and burning witches. Scientific ideas are not published mainly to benefit the ego of the investigator but to expose the ideas to the test of others, to allow them to detect errors, and to allow as many people as possible to think of opportunities for further steps. There is no identifiable closed circle of people who can guarantee the creation of scientific insights or detect errors in them. Einstein, after all, was once a mere examiner in the Swiss patent office with no official recognition and no top-secret clearance.

Public policy, even more than science, is likely to be perfected by involvment with the many rather than with the few. Few scientific pursuits are as complex and subtle as formulating a public policy that is appropriate for 200 million Americans or, more demanding still, for more than 4 billion human beings and the interlocked interests of their 160 nations. Giving citizens access to the processes and information of government is not merely an elegant flourish in the Declaration of Independence. It is the only way that a national consensus can be reached in a viable and continuing way, which is to say, the only way democracy can succeed and endure.

Secrecy and censorship remove the vital information from the political process. The smaller the circle of knowledge, the greater the incidence of undetected error and of detachment from reality. The sequestered decision making of the elite has produced a succession of catastrophes in the history of the twentieth century, from World War I to Vietnam. If information is withheld because it is considered too disturbing for the public, it merely postpones society's confrontation with its problem. It removes the issue from open, political resolution.

Even secrecy considered justified, the atom bomb project during World War II, nevertheless had a high, subsequent cost. Atomic secrecy after the war made it possible to conceal the effects of low-level radiation, permitted political exploitation for massive military spending to close alleged gaps—"missile" and "bomber" and "windows of vulnerability"—that later were found to be nonexistent, withheld data that led to fateful decisions to make hydrogen bombs, and let Cold War and McCarthyist cynicism persecute people such as J. Robert Oppenheimer, who helped create the secrets in the first place.

The vast apparatus of secrecy in the United States, which began more than a generation ago, is now so large that no one any longer knows how many documents are classified or even how many thousands of government and industrial functionaries have the power to stamp documents secret. Even classifiers admit that most of what is stamped secret could safely be made public. No one has been able to find a way to discover the documents that may be needed for history that are in the tons of sealed papers. Periodically, a government leader with a sense of obligation to the ethic of democracy tries to slow the pace, to move toward a more open government. The Freedom of Information Act was passed to give the citizen some limited right to the information possessed by his government. Occasionally, an attempt is made to reduce the size of the army of people permitted to classify documents. These attempts have been reversed by President Reagan. The Freedom of Information Act has been made more restrictive. Secrecy and censorship have been spread to areas of government and scholarship never before hidden from the public. These and other acts of excluding the citizens from their government usually are accomplished in innocuously numbered "Executive Orders" or little-publicized bureaucratic reorganizations. Two hundred years ago, James Madison issued a warning appropriate for our time: "I believe there are more instances of the abridgment of the freedom of the people by gradual and silent encroachment of those in power than by violent and sudden usurpation."

BEN H. BAGDIKIAN
Author of *The Media Monopoly*
Graduate School of Journalism,
University of California, Berkeley

KEEPING AMERICA
UNINFORMED

Chapter 1

INTRODUCTION

In 1982, representatives of the ultrasecret National Security Agency paid a visit to the George C. Marshall Research Library, a nonprofit private library at the Virginia Military Institute in Lexington, Virginia. Their mission was to sequester documents that had been used by James Bamford in writing his unauthorized study of the NSA titled *The Puzzle Palace*, published the same year. This remarkable event was the result of a presidential order that for the first time in American history gave the federal government the right to reclassify material that had already been declassified—in this instance for as long as twenty years—and was sitting on library shelves open to the public. Bamford later commented that his was "the only book in history to have been totally unclassified as it was being written, yet top secret by the time it was published."

The presidential order that permitted reclassification was but part of an historic change that has been taking place regarding the government's handling of information. During the last several years, actions taken by the government have resulted in a dramatic increase in government secrecy and a severe reduction in public access to information. The Reagan administration's great penchant for secrecy has permeated government action at all levels. At the start of 1984, the press reported that the administration had been

3

concealing an unknown number of small-scale nuclear tests for at least a year, quietly breaking with a 1975 policy requiring that all such tests be made public.[1] Shortly before this story broke, the Department of Energy had announced plans to restrict the availability of unclassified information about the research and development of nuclear weapons.[2] The Office of Management and Budget has tried to preempt public debate on controversial issues by proposing a rule that would prohibit all political advocacy by groups receiving federal funds.[3]

In addition, the Reagan administration has accelerated the government's abandonment of its role as a primary provider of information. Ever since the New Deal in the 1930's, and especially in the 1960's and 1970's, as the government has taken a more active role in society it has become a clearinghouse for vital information for many diverse elements of the population. It has become an important and sometimes the only source of data on such general topics as transportation, agriculture, and education. The flow of information among government entities and to the public has become the mortar of our society.

Reagan's priorities of secrecy and curtailment of government provision of information derive from his fundamental belief that the chief obligation of government is national defense and that other federal activities should be kept to a minimum. In accordance with this philosophy, his administration has severely restricted public access to information, keeping America uninformed and thereby endangering the foundation of democratic government.

This book recounts recent modifications in federal information policy that highlight the significance of increasing government control. As defined here, "federal information policy" encompasses the standards established for the classification of federal documents; regulatory procedures that help or hinder public awareness; statistical programs; and government production of publications, computer tapes, and audiovisual material. Information policy also includes political criteria applied to foreign films, publications, and visa permits; laws regarding individual privacy; and governmentwide actions that touch upon First Amendment principles affecting the circulation of information and ideas. There is, in fact, not one unified federal information policy but a decentralized structure involved in hundreds of programs. Nonetheless, in each president's administration, standards and objectives are developed that, to varying degrees, affect the fundamental issues of open government and individual freedom.

The Reagan administration's restrictive information policy has been based on three principal objectives. The first has been deregulation of business. In the 1960's and 1970's, the expansion of regulation in new areas of social concern produced a large increase in the circulation of information among regulatory agencies, business corporations, and the public. For the first time, large quantities of information became available to ordinary citizens. Of course, new form-filing requirements included in regulations imposed new burdens on industry, state and local governments, and other entities. Federal paperwork became the target of complaints that were later a central part of Reagan's plans to streamline the federal government. One company's paperwork burden, however, is another person's vital source of information about such matters as workplace disabilities and environmental hazards. The deregulatory policies of the Reagan administration have left important gaps in public knowledge about vital issues of concern.

The second objective of the administration's information policy has been to narrow the information-related responsibilities of the government. Previously, the federal government had provided information needed by local governments, business, social-service professionals, and other groups for whom the collection and analysis of information on a nationwide basis was impractical. The Reagan administration has acted to transfer many of these activities to the private sector.

Efforts to "privatize," or contract out, government programs are not new. Throughout the 1970's, there was much talk of possible ways to trim the operations of government. Toward the end of his term, President Jimmy Carter urged federal agencies to contract out many of their operations.

In this regard, information presents unique considerations. The traditional emphasis on keeping information in the public domain, especially where it touches upon the operations of government, reflects the dependence of a democratic society on a well-informed citizenry. Hence, government actions that restrict the availability of information are of paramount importance. Even the strongest proponents of placing government activities under private jurisdiction have tended to see central information activities as public goods. For example, Emanuel S. Savas, former assistant secretary of the Department of Housing and Urban Development, has said in his book *Privatizing the Public Sector* that broadcasting, like national defense, is a collective rather than a private good.[4] In contrast, the Reagan administration, represented by the chairman of the Federal Communications Commission, Mark Fowler, has recommended auctioning off the airwaves. The Reagan administration also tried unsuccessfully to sell the nation's weather satellites, another primary source of information.

Interestingly, the private sector has opposed the administration's plans in certain areas of ostensible profitability. Donald Woolley, chief economist of Banker's Trust, testifying before Congress in 1982, criticized agency cutbacks in the gathering and analysis of statistics, stating that federal numbers were "the only aggregate data available for analyzing national economic trends" and could not be replaced by private efforts.[5]

The third objective of the administration's information

policy has been control of the parameters of political debate. By denying or avoiding facts and restricting essential information, the administration has sought to shield itself from the glare of public scrutiny. Protecting national security has been a catch-all rationale for these actions.

Nearly everyone would agree that some information should be withheld to protect the nation's vital interests. At times, the threat to national security is visible and immediate, as when military codes must be protected during wartime. Most of these instances have been addressed through legislation since the beginning of this century. In other instances, however, the threats to the nation are not so palpable. Then it is necessary to distinguish attempts to save face or avoid public scrutiny from legitimate national-security interests. The determination as to whether material should be released depends on how national security is defined and how the objective of open government is balanced with the need for secrecy in specific instances.

Presidents and government agencies have frequently engaged in tugs of war with Congress and the courts over what information they were required to reveal. Information can be withheld in many different ways. Presidents have been known to refuse to share documents with Congress— at times asserting executive privilege—to stonewall requests, to deny the existence of requested documents, and to tell outright lies. Perhaps the leading practitioner of these techniques was Richard Nixon, whose battles over disclosure played an important part in his eventual political demise. Despite these occasions, since World War II, there have been significant advances toward more open government. The Reagan years, however, have seen a major setback to that trend. Not only has Reagan returned to some of the most injurious practices of past presidents, he has also enacted a series of restrictions on information that, taken together, constitute a major assault on the Constitution.

The following chapters describe recent government actions that have limited the availability of information. These restrictions have had an adverse impact on many groups, including universities, unions, private businesses, the scientific community, and the environmental movement. In many instances, the government has ensured that new limitations will outlast the current administration by incorporating them in directives, laws, and agency regulations. It is not simple to find the best way to modify such restrictions. For example, in 1983, Congress enacted legislation prohibiting the requirements, established by a presidential directive earlier that year, that government officials take lie detector tests and submit speeches and manuscripts for review prior to publication. This congressional action did not, however, cover all such nondisclosure agreements, and, while many people thought the problem solved, the administration continued to circulate nondisclosure contracts.

The next chapter focuses on the White House and discusses aspects of Reagan's policies in the economic and political spheres that bear upon public access to information. His mistrust of public scrutiny of the government, especially by the media, has led to new restrictions and the strengthening of previous ones.

Chapter 3 considers the Office of Management and Budget, which has taken a strong role in implementing the government's deregulatory and budgetary objectives. In the course of this activity, the OMB has been afforded superagency status, enabling it to intervene in programs of agencies of the executive branch. On numerous occasions, it has seemed to come into conflict with congressional objectives.

Chapter 4 turns to the regulatory agencies, which have also reduced the flow of information to the public. Reagan's appointed agency chiefs have fired consumer-affairs personnel, reoriented public information bureaus to serve business interests, and eliminated many publications that provided necessary information to the public. In addition, in most agencies, requests filed under the Freedom of Information Act (FOIA) meet with long delays and sharply increased fees. Essential agency resources of data on specialized topics have been weakened through attrition of personnel, budget cuts, and, on occasion, the contracting out of agency libraries.

Chapter 5 on Congress reveals that it too has enacted restrictive measures. A recent law makes it a crime today to publicize the identities of U.S. intelligence officers, even when it is already in the public domain. Each year, new FOIA exemptions have been created, sometimes unannounced. Congressional activity pales, however, in comparison with the systematic efforts of the executive branch to thwart access to information. Furthermore, Congress has often been the victim of the administration's policies. Cabinet-level agencies such as the Department of Interior have refused to bow to the oversight functions of Congress until threatened with subpoenas and court action. Lengthy preliminary negotiations and much paperwork have often been necessary to bring about the desired agency cooperation with routine requests by congressional committees for information.

The discussion in chapter 6 centers on the media, which have been the subject of carefully laid plans by high-ranking Reagan officials to restrict contact with government personnel and to diminish the usefulness of the Freedom of Information Act. In 1983, a Federal Bureau of Investigation (FBI) official who spoke with reporters about the bureau's plans to investigate the Cartergate incident—the acquisition of Carter camp documents by Reagan supporters during the 1980 presidential campaign—was abruptly transferred from Washington, D.C., to Portland, Oregon, after his statements appeared in print. In another attempt to control leaks, the president adopted a directive in 1983 requiring all federal employees with access to classified information to submit speeches and writings for prior screening. An ambitious attempt to introduce a law-enforcement system within the bureaucracy, the directive has been temporarily suspended, first by Congress, and then by President Reagan.

Chapter 7 describes recent attempts to impose secrecy restrictions on scientific research on grounds of national security. The administration has diminished free scientific inquiry by applying export controls to the teaching of science, the publication of unclassified research, and university instruction to foreign students. It has also sought to curtail exchanges of information in international conferences.

The government functions as a primary resource in the provision of statistical information, the subject of chapter 8. Today, more than ninety different government entities are involved in the preparation of data that are used for economic planning, housing programs, and various other purposes. Federal numbers are used to chart literacy rates, unemployment, economic deficits, and the quality of life. This chapter looks at actions taken by Congress and other users of federal statistics to impress upon Reagan officials the importance to the private sector, nonprofit organizations, local government, and federal agencies of unimpaired federal statistical programs.

The library community, discussed in chapter 9, is perhaps the group that is most aware of the radical nature of current changes in government information policy. The widened classification rules and Reagan's overall penchant for secrecy conflict with longstanding library traditions upholding public access to information. Hundreds of public and specialized libraries rely upon the government for their materials and have, at the very least, been inconvenienced by increased fees for government publications, the elimination of federal information products, and other changes.

The last two chapters contain the author's conclusions

and a directory of organizations concerned with maintaining open government.

At stake here is what David Bender, executive director of the Special Libraries Association, has called the "collective memory" of our society. If government abandons its basic information functions, how will progress be measured? How will history be remembered? Specific criteria are needed for determining whether information functions should be privatized or limited in circulation. More than ever, the issue of access to information is central to the future of popular government.

Chapter 2

THE TIGHT-LIPPED PRESIDENCY

The Imperial Presidency, a recurring phenomenon in American politics, was discredited in the Watergate period only to return in the 1980's. Ronald Reagan built upon the actions of previous presidents in consolidating power in the Oval Office and downplaying the role of Congress. Challenging long-standing constitutional traditions of open public debate, he developed policies characterized by a bias toward secrecy, great intolerance of dissident public movements, and a preoccupation with molding public opinion. In foreign policy, his near-exclusive emphasis on anti-Communism returned the country to a situation reminiscent of the 1950's when the assertion of United States ideological supremacy prompted the government to intervene regularly in foreign conflicts and to intimidate critics at home. Additionally, in his crusade to reorganize the federal government, he set about to reorient the regulatory agencies to the needs of business. One of the results of this new policy was a drastic reduction in the information made available by the agencies to the public.

Managing Political Debate

Reagan had, in the years before he entered the Oval Office, developed a substantial amount of public relations skill through his acting career and his experience working as a good will ambassador for the General Electric Corporation. During his administration, he has often applied this expertise to "making the truth attractive"—the president's own description of the way topics likely to produce controversy should be presented. One of the main obstacles to accomplishing this aim, according to Reagan, is the unauthorized disclosure of information by current and former government officials. Reagan has taken extraordinary measures to control leaks and restrict access to sensitive information.

Secrecy Through Classification

The first presidential order on classification was issued by Franklin Delano Roosevelt in 1940. Executive Order 8381 and those that followed set the basic rules for the classification of documents by government agencies. Roosevelt relied on a 1938 law concerning the security of armed forces installations and "information relative thereto" to justify his action. However, according to a 1982 report on security classification policy of the House Committee on Government Operations, the legislative history of the 1938 law contained no indication that the presidential classification authority asserted by Roosevelt was intended by Congress.[1] Since that time, the basis of the presidential classification orders promulgated by Dwight Eisenhower, Richard Nixon, Jimmy Carter, and Reagan has been in dispute. The scope of classification has gradually widened from an almost exclusive focus on the military to matters of economic and technological security. As the focus has expanded, there have been many calls for direction from Congress that would, at the very least, set parameters for regulation based on the "national security" and designate categories of information eligible for classification.

From the early 1950's until the Reagan years, the trend was toward limiting the volume of, and setting time limits on, material subject to classification. In 1972, Nixon issued Executive Order 11652, which made several significant changes in the order that had been adopted by Eisenhower and revised by Kennedy. Nixon substantially reduced the number of personnel who could review government information for classification. Timetables ranging from six to thirty years were set for the automatic declassification of documents. For the first time, a private citizen was given the right to request review of classification continued past the deadline set forth in the order for declassification.

The Carter administration's Executive Order on Security Classification, 12065, was the first to list specific categories and thereby limit the type of information subject to classification. Material subject to classification had to fall in one of seven categories. Previous orders had only provided vague standards for classification in terms of the damage that would result from disclosure. In addition to providing these categories, the Carter order was the first one to confine classification to documents that could reasonably be expected to cause "identifiable damage" to the national security if released.

The special efforts made by the Carter administration to limit needless classification were described in a letter from Richard M. Neustadt, an author of the Carter order, to a House subcommittee in 1982. He conveyed Carter's concern that overclassfication undermines respect for overall security protection. To deal with this issue, the interagency team appointed to draft the classification order received extensive comment on draft versions from such people as constitutional experts, interested congressional committees, and civil servants, who were most often the ones to make classification determinations. Neustadt's letter left little doubt that the final product benefited considerably from this process.[2] The Reagan order, by contrast, according to a House committee report, failed "fully [to] inform Congress and the public about the proposal to change security classification rules or to solicit advice at a meaningful time during the revision process."[3] Those involved in the drafting phase did not meet with members of Congress until after Reagan had signed the order.

Yet another important provision in the Carter order was one that required the application of a balancing test to determine whether classified information could be released. The order stated: "In some cases, the need to protect such information may be outweighed by the public interest in disclosure of the information, and in these cases, the information should be declassified. When such questions arise, they shall be referred to the agency head, a senior agency official with responsibility for processing Freedom of Information Act requests. . . ."

This provision allowed agency officials discretion to evaluate requests for information according to particular circumstances, a procedure of particular importance for Freedom of Information Act (FOIA) requests. Under the terms of the FOIA,[4] documents can be withheld only if they meet the substantive and procedural criteria of the current executive order on classification. The ad hoc balancing test and emphasis on disclosure in the Carter order made the FOIA a stronger law.

The Carter order was seen as a step toward greater accountability for the classifying agent; the Reagan order went in the direction of increased classification and less public accountability. The Carter balancing test was eliminated, as was the requirement that documents be found likely to cause identifiable damage before they could be classified. Additionally, any doubts regarding different levels of classification were to be resolved by stamping documents at the highest level of nondisclosure. Finally, Reagan's order discarded previous executive order provisions mandating systematic review and declassification.[5]

The elimination of the balancing test was given special attention when Reagan officials testified before Congress in the spring of 1982. Upon close questioning, Steven Garfinkel, director of the Information Security and Oversight Office, stated that reference to the balancing test had been eliminated because "balancing is *inherently* a part of the decision to classify and declassify information." This answer only provoked an additional question: If the issue was inherent, why was the reference removed?

According to Richard K. Willard, deputy assistant attorney general at the Department of Justice, who later was revealed to be the principal author of a March 1983 directive requiring more than 120,000 federal employees to sign secrecy agreements, the balancing reference had been removed to clarify the court's power to review FOIA decisions. The FOIA requires disclosure of government documents if it would serve the public interest. According to the Reagan administration, when FOIA decisions were appealed, courts were not to judge the validity of the public interest determinations made by federal agencies. The executive order's elimination of the balancing test as a matter of record was intended to emphasize this limitation.

The scope of judicial review over the FOIA cannot be decided by the White House alone. Courts also look to relevant congressional history and the Constitution. However, Reagan's order to agency personnel to downplay—if not abandon—the public interest issue meant that many fewer documents would be declassified. Also, since courts generally have been deferential toward executive orders based on reasons of national security, Reagan's order made things more difficult for anyone seeking to challenge an agency decision.

Additionally, the elimination of the Carter requirement that potential damage be identified to justify classification removed an important procedural check on abuse of the authority to classify. As underscored by former Central Intelligence Agency agent Victor Marchetti in his book *CIA and the Cult of Intelligence,* the motivation for classifica-

tion very often is related more to hiding embarrassing information than protecting real state secrets.

Further, the Reagan order eliminated an earlier restriction against reclassification. The Carter order had stated
that "classification may not be restored to documents already declassified and released to the public under the Freedom of Information Act." Reagan's order authorized classifying information at any time and specifically, in the
course of reviewing FOIA requests, so long as the information required protection in the interest of national security
and could be recovered without extraordinary measures
taken. These conditions were so vague as to be almost in-
consequential.

The effect of such reclassification authority can be seen
in the previously mentioned instance of James Bamford's
problems with the NSA. Although many of the documents
he used had been declassified for two to three decades and
had appeared in print in more than 150,000 copies of Bamford's book, the NSA insisted that the information was still
secret and the documents should therefore be reclassified.
Indeed, the director of the NSA, James Faurer, noted that
"just because information has been published doesn't mean
it should no longer be classified." Of some importance,
NSA's action occurred after the Reagan order had been
signed but before it went into effect. Hence, Faurer's statement was a reflection of the power his agency had arrogated
unto itself outside the law.

More ominously, officials at the NSA instructed librarians at the Virginia Military Institute to withhold certain
materials that Bamford had used in his research. Reagan's
executive order and similar documents limit classification
to material "that is owned by, produced by or for, or is
under the control of the United States Government." Yet
the NSA reached out to suppress information held outside
the government by a private library. Much of the library's
material of interest to NSA consisted of letters to and from

private citizens about family matters dating from 1955 to 1965. It is difficult to see how these notes could damage national security.

The new reclassification authority means that the current and future administrations now have the power to revise history when the facts are unfavorable—a situation not unlike the Ministry of Truth in George Orwell's novel *Nineteen Eighty-four*. As happened in Virginia, history can be pulled off the shelf and out of public view, leaving the public with only its own fragile memory.

Reagan's War on the Unauthorized Disclosure of Information

It is the aim of all leaders to present a unified front. Nonetheless, in every presidential administration, attempts to suppress unwanted disclosures have met with imperfect success. Each federal agency has its own agenda and, from time to time, will deliberately share inside information that conflicts with White House intentions in order to muster support for its own position. Such behavior rarely is truly subversive. More often, it is simply the cause of intensified public debate.

Reagan, believing that any trace of employee disloyalty justified intensified surveillance, declared war on leaks early on. New restrictions were imposed on all contacts between agency personnel and the media. In an effort to reduce the visibility of the Central Intelligence Agency, a long-standing agency policy of formally briefing reporters about nonclassified information was eliminated in 1981. Two years later, Reagan ordered his own staff in the White House to take lie detector tests after the press unexpectedly reported plans of military action in Lebanon. In addition, each year the White House proposed legislation intended to weaken significantly the FOIA. These actions attracted attention from Congress, which asked responsible federal officials to testify on the administration's intentions. Rather unexpectedly, two days of hearings revealed that the number of unauthorized disclosures had not risen in the 1980's. Steven Garfinkel of the Information Security and Oversight Office reported only six to ten serious leaks between 1980 and 1983.

Reagan did not hide his strong suspicion of, and resentment toward, the media. His animosity dated back to the role they played during the Vietnam War, when nightly pictures from Asia on television brought home scenes of casualties and devastation. Reagan and many of his closest advisers saw this display as the main reason for the erosion of public support for the war at that time. Consequently, Reagan regarded the media as a likely foe of any attempt to muster support for U.S. military activity abroad. From the outset, as seen during the invasion of Grenada in 1983, his administration vigilantly monitored the media's coverage of the government, paying special attention to television. Wayward newscasters were often notified of White House disapproval.

The president's preoccupation with leaks was much broader than the media. His executive order on classification was aimed at information that had been declassified during more liberal administrations and might again be released. More generally, Reagan put national security and the loyalty of his officials above all other values. His policies were modeled accordingly. As Floyd Abrams, a prominent First Amendment lawyer, has stated, "The Administration's fixation, as I view it, on national security at the expense of freedom of expression is such that it seems virtually always to require the latter claims to be overcome, even when those claims are at their greatest and the needs of national security are at their least compelling."[6] Reagan's position challenged two hundred years of Constitutional history.

In March of 1983, Reagan put his own First Amendment

views on the line by introducing a sweeping system of prior restraint. National Security Directive 84, more than any order or regulation in U.S. history, institutionalized executive control over officials' speech.[7] How much censorship would Congress, government officials, and the courts tolerate in the name of national security?

The directive required first that all current and former officials with access to classified information, no matter how low the level of classification, sign nondisclosure agreements. Second, it required those with access to extrasensitive material to sign similar agreements, except that contracts developed for this august group were to include provisions for prepublication review of all speeches and writings that touched upon classified information, even when the author relied entirely on public documents. Both of these groups had to agree to undergo lie detector tests when leaks were being investigated. The implications of the lie detector and prior-review requirements are discussed below, following a description of the directive's enforcement procedure.

Each government agency was to set up internal procedures to evaluate unauthorized disclosures and administer lie detector examinations. Agencies originally responsible for marking documents classified were to be brought in to assist these investigations. After agency examinations, the names of suspect employees were to be reported to the Justice Department, which, in turn, could seek an FBI investigation. The directive indicated that separate agency agreements with the FBI would be permitted. Finally, a provision of the directive allowed civil court actions in addition to criminal investigations to be brought against those suspected of contract violations. Government victories won in court against Frank Snepp and other former intelligence agents who had signed nondisclosure contracts had instructed the White House on the utility of civil penalties. These measures clearly went way beyond previous attempts to prevent the disclosure of sensitive intelligence information. As the American Jewish Committee stated in a submission to Congress, "the scope of the Directive is so broad as to create a potentially vast censorship system the purpose of which may be unrelated to legitimate national security."

PREPUBLICATION REVIEW

The prepublication-review provision of the National Security Directive applied to all writings, including books (even novels), reports, studies, articles, columns, lecture notes, speeches, letters to the editor, and book reviews. Prior review was mandated whether or not any classified material was included in an author's writing, on the assumption that only the agency itself could determine whether classified information would be disclosed by the publication. This catchall requirement continued after the person was no longer employed by the government.

As noted by the Association of American Publishers, such government review "cannot help but have a pronounced chilling effect on the publishing process and a devastating impact on informed public discussion which is at the heart of our system of democratic government." One of the most damaging aspects of the directive was the likelihood that experienced, knowledgeable people would shy away from public discussion of matters where their expertise was greatest. Fewer people would be willing to enter government for short periods of time when, rather than having greater opportunities to influence policy discussion, they would be subject to indefinite surveillance and lie detector examinations. The directive also meant less timely coverage of important issues since it required that news stories and columns written by someone who had worked in government be submitted for government review before being printed.

Robert Lewis, chairman of the National Freedom of Information Committee of the Society of Professional Journalists, testifying before the Senate Judiciary Committee, asked if the directive could really be in the public interest if it meant that speeches and writings of former government officials would be reviewed by their successors. For example, he said, in theory, vice presidential candidate George Bush would have needed to have all his campaign speeches cleared with the Carter administration if the Reagan directive had existed in 1979. Similarly, had the directive not been suspended by Congress, presidential candidate Walter Mondale would have had to submit his campaign speeches to Reagan-appointed review boards.

Key political commentators are perpetually at risk under these conditions. The columns and articles of such people as Leslie Gelb, Jody Powell, and William F. Buckley, Jr., theoretically, could all be subject to prior review. The absurdity of this situation was summed up by Charles W. Maynes, journalist and former State Department employee, who stated: "A speech given three weeks after the vote is not a relevant speech. An article delivered 30 days after the attention of the nation has moved to another item is not a printable article. In the past three years I, myself, have probably written 40 major articles for the nation's leading newspapers. Subjects have ranged from El Salvador to South Africa to the Soviet Union. I can't think of more than one or two of these articles that I, as an editor, would have considered publishable a month after the editors of the newspapers in question requested them. Yet precisely someone like myself would be subject to the new regulations, as I have served in the executive branch and subsequently embarked on a career as editor and commentator."

In systems of prior review, there is great potential for the suppression of dissident points of view. Not surprisingly, during the Reagan years, prior-review procedures were applied selectively. Many former intelligence agents have been invited to sign nondisclosure agreements that existed before the March directive. Many have refused to sign or to submit to prepublication review, including Buckley and E. Howard Hunt. As might be expected, those supportive of the Reagan government have been left alone. The inherent dangers in this selective enforcement scheme threaten the foundation of a pluralistic society.

LIE DETECTOR TESTS

In 1983, of an estimated 5 million federal civilian and military employees, almost one-half had access to some level of classified information and were subject to the National Security Directive. Additionally, approximately 1.5 million federal contractors with access to classified materials might also be asked to sign one of the nondisclosure agreements. The March directive made all of these employees and contractors potential candidates for lie detector examinations.

The lie detector requirement most dramatically reveals the similarity between the March directive and the surveillance mechanisms of a police state that parades the confessions of a "state enemy" obtained under duress.

One of the primary reasons for strong opposition to the lie detector test is that the lie detector, or polygraph, is not regarded as a scientific instrument. Numerous experiments conducted during the past ten years have shown that it detects nervousness and excitement more than truth, thus casting serious doubt on its reliability as a means of establishing truth or falsity. On October 19, 1983, Dr. John H. Gibbons, director of the Congressional Office of Technology Assessment, presented the results of an OTA study of polygraphs at a congressional hearing. He testified that "there is no scientific evidence to establish the validity of polygraph screening for a large number of people in connection with the investigation of unauthorized disclosures." He further noted that no research had yet been done on the use of polygraphs to conduct initial screenings as was envisioned in the Reagan directive. Very different results were likely to emerge in this situation, which lacked the conventional preliminary investigation used to detect prime suspects in criminal situations.

Richard K. Willard, the main author of the March directive, admitted that "the polygraph itself does not detect lies. The polygraph is an instrument that measures a variety of physiological responses." Nonetheless, he maintained that polygraphs would assist the examiner in forming an opinion as to an individual's credibility.

Another reason for opposition is the largely subjective nature of polygraph testing. The test requires the examiner to infer truth or falsity based on a comparison of a person's physiological responses to a series of questions. The questions posed depend on whatever information the examiner already has about the person being tested. Personality factors clearly play a large role in the entire procedure.

Willard claimed that the overwhelming majority of studies showed accuracy rates within the range of 70 to 95 percent. Gibbons, however, disagreed. The OTA study had confirmed the results of other polygraph tests, which showed a very wide range of accuracy, with correct detections frequently ranging as low as 17 percent.

Because of serious doubts concerning the reliability of polygraphs, federal courts do not treat such information as admissible evidence. The use of these tests on federal employees who have not been charged with any offense, in effect, treats the innocent as guilty, at the same time that allegedly guilty persons are protected. Significantly, when asked at a press conference if he would sign a nondisclosure agreement, Reagan declined. By late 1983, every high-level official in his Cabinet had followed the president's example.

The Reagan directive and similar restrictions have little chance of catching people who truly endanger the nation's interests. Such people are unlikely to sign nondisclosure forms or to write about their activities. Instead, this type of restriction will serve to harass people of good intentions and damage traditions of free speech. The directive's misdirectedness is its final and fatal flaw.

In the fall of 1983, after extensive hearings on both the polygraph and prior-review requirements, Congress passed legislation prohibiting enforcement of these provisions of the directive until April 1984. Much stronger countermeasures would have been justified. Moreover, this action did not encompass all of the nondisclosure agreements that were being imposed within federal agencies at that time. The need for permanent limitations on the use of such agreements is clear. In March 1984, Reagan agreed to suspend parts of the directive, including those covering prior-review and lie detector agreements, until the end of the year. This action was received with much excitement, although its significance was misread. During an election year, great efforts are made by all the presidential candidates to obscure the rough edges of their prior records. The pullback on the directive was a transparent attempt to remove the directive as a sticking point in Senate hearings on the confirmation of Edwin Meese as U.S. attorney general and as a presidential election issue. The temporary suspension of the directive was clear evidence of Reagan's plan to move forward on it at a later date.

FOREIGN POLICY

Information is a vital component in the conduct of a nation's foreign affairs. During the twentieth century, the growth of intelligence agencies and overseas public relations offices, under the auspices of the United States Information Agency, has put the collection and management of information at the center of foreign policy. Reagan has carried this trend even further than other administrations and has embarked on an explicit war of ideas with what he has called the Soviet "evil empire." In addition to disseminating U.S. propaganda abroad, he has attempted to control the entry of unattractive foreign ideas into the United States.

Bans on Publications and Travel

The administration has increased limitations on the entry of foreign publications from perceived enemy countries into the United States. Cuba has been the key target of this type of restriction. In May of 1981, after nearly twenty years of an uninterrupted flow of written materials from Cuba, the U.S. government seized thousands of publications that had been mailed to the United States. It claimed that it was acting under the authority of regulations issued pursuant to the Trading with the Enemy Act, which, since 1963, had required a license for goods imported from Cuba. These regulations had never been enforced against periodicals before. The First Amendment encourages the free flow of information and exposure to competing ideas and information; except in times of war, it has been understood to rule out this type of censorship.

Around the same time that periodicals were prohibited, regulations were issued that banned business and tourist travel to Cuba. This action was soon challenged in court and overruled. The government also has imposed restrictions on university professors and scientists attending conferences overseas and on meetings in this country involving people of the same profession from different places. At the crux of these restrictions is a debate (discussed more fully in chapter 7) between the government and security officials over the extent to which security restrictions should be applied to scientific knowledge. The Reagan administration's position has been that the transfer of technological and other types of information encourages the Soviet Union's massive military ambitions. Other groups, such as the National Academy of Sciences, maintain that the government's restrictions on research and travel could be extremely damaging to overall scientific and military progress and that the national security is more apt to be enhanced through a policy of open communication that promotes scientific achievement in military and civilian life. Laws and regulations limiting the exchange of ideas swiftly chill the instinct to pioneer new inventions.

Project Democracy

The administration also sought to involve other nations in its plans to spread democratic values. In a speech to the British Parliament in 1982, Reagan called for Project Democracy, a unified campaign to "foster the infrastructure of democracy—the system of a free press, unions, political parties, universities—which allows a people to choose their own way, to develop their own culture, to reconcile their own differences, through peaceful means." Soon after, he asked Congress to allocate more than $65 million in the coming year to teach the world about democracy. Secretary of State George Shultz testified that "Project Democracy" had five components, including some forty-four separate proposals for seminars, institutes, publications, and fellowships abroad. The administration planned to seek active involvement by private organizations and leaders, including labor unions and major corporations. In addition, a substantial increase in funds was requested for Radio Free Europe, the U.S. Information Agency, and other branches of overseas government information operations, which had already been significantly expanded during the preceding two years.

At least one part of Project Democracy was directed at the U.S. population. Senior White House officials informed Congress that increased surveillance of antinuclear organizations would be conducted with project funding. Because the full scope of White House plans for this program was outlined in a classified, top-secret executive order, it was unclear what other domestic groups had been targeted.[8]

Other Restrictive Policies

In general, Reagan exhibited little tolerance for free-wheeling public debate. He was especially critical of the movement opposing the placement of nuclear missiles in Western Europe, calling its adherents "anti-nuclear terrorists," and of objections to the administration's operations in Latin America. On several occasions, foreign films not fully in accordance with administration policies, were labled "political propaganda" by the Department of Justice. For example, in 1983, *If You Love This Planet,* a Canadian film about the medical effects of nuclear war, along with two other Canadian films about acid rain, were put in this category under a provision of the Foreign Agents Registration Act. In addition, temporary visas were denied to such foreigners as Mrs. Salvador Allende, Gabriel Garcia Marquez, and Japanese survivors of Hiroshima on the grounds that their speeches to U.S. audiences would not be in the public interest.

The administration's attempts to mold public opinion included several known instances of blatant fabrication. In February 1981, two months after the start of the Reagan government, the State Department issued a White Paper entitled "Communist Interference in El Salvador," an eight-page, single-spaced document that "presents definitive evidence of the clandestine military support given by the Soviet Union, Cuba and their Communist allies to overthrow the established Government of El Salvador." Supposedly, this information had been "drawn from captured guerrilla documents and war material." The White Paper was picked up by every wire service and big city newspaper in the country. Yet, within a short time, it was found to contain numerous factual errors, unsupported assertions, and misstatements. After six months of inquiries conducted in different quarters, the State Department backed down, admitting that it could not vouch for most of the White Paper's information.

The Salvadoran incident was only one of several similar mishaps in the early 1980's. Of course, the White Paper drama resembled similar incidents in earlier administrations, most notably the discovery that the Johnson and Nixon governments had misrepresented the truth during the Vietnam War. The Reagan administration appears no different in this regard. History, however, may show this president, so gifted in public relations, to have been the most skillful at creating the news.

REORIENTATION OF THE REGULATORY AGENCIES

One of the main ways in which information restrictions have been implemented has been the withdrawal of several of the federal regulatory agencies from the provision of information to the public. In several instances, Reagan's appointed agency directors established for their agencies new priorities that interrupted the exchange of information with public groups and concentrated on serving the interests of corporate entities.

The Paperwork Reduction Act of 1980

The administration's actions in the area of regulation relied in large measure on the Paperwork Reduction Act of 1980. Beginning in the 1970's a recent large expansion in government regulation produced an opposition movement, comprised mainly of businesses and local governments, which complained, in part, about federal intervention through form filing and other information-related requirements. In response to this protest, in 1974, Congress established a bi-partisan Commission on Federal Paperwork, headed by Rep. Frank Horton, to investigate the paperwork burdens that had come along with increasing agency responsibilities. Two years later, the commission concluded that the cost of federal paperwork was indeed excessive, amounting to more than $100 billion a year, much of it the result of sloppy management and conflicting agency assignments. Building on commission recommendations, Congress then enacted the Paperwork Reduction Act of 1980.

This act set a goal of reducing the amount of information collected by the government by 25 percent within three years. Each agency was to designate a senior official who would be responsible for seeing that information activities were executed in a more efficient manner. Overseeing the entire project was the Office of Management and Budget, with primary responsibilities centered in a new Office of Information and Regulatory Affairs (OIRA) located in the OMB. The enormous scope of this legislation was evident from the OMB director's mandate to "develop and implement Federal information policies" and "to review information collection requests, the reduction of the paperwork burden, Federal statistical activities, [and] privacy of records," in addition to directing the introduction of new data-processing technology. The majority of these functions were to be carried out by OIRA, which soon became the nucleus of the Reagan administration's information policies.

Once in office, Reagan continued the concern over paperwork burdens, making it a featured aspect of his crusade to discipline and restrict the activity of the regulatory agencies.

In his second month, he announced the creation of a White House Task Force on Regulatory Relief, headed by Vice President Bush. Its task was to review all regulatory proposals, "particularly those burdensome to the national economy or key industrial sectors." About the same time, the president also issued Executive Order 12291, which centralized management of executive branch agencies in the OMB.[10] The Paperwork Reduction Act had extended the OMB's responsibilities considerably, giving it power to oversee the collection and dissemination of information. Reagan's order then made the OMB a superagency by making all new regulatory initiatives in the executive branch contingent upon OMB approval. Before any new proposal could be announced in the *Federal Register,* the customary way of informing public groups, it had to be placed before the OMB, which could then request changes, hold the proposal indefinitely, or grant approval. In this way, there was prior screening by the OMB before word could get out that might evoke counterpressures to its own deregulatory objectives.

Underlying this executive order and numerous subsequent OMB circulars, was the president's belief that the federal government should model itself after business. Reagan envisioned a sort of holding company arrangement, with all agency planning and budgetary activity cleared through the White House and the OMB. In 1983, "Reform 88," a six-year effort to restructure the administrative systems of the federal government, was launched. OMB Deputy Director Joseph Wright told the press that the goal of this project was to make the government operate as efficiently "as an Exxon."[11]

Like the Carter and Nixon administrations, the Reagan government sought greater control over the activities of the regulatory agencies and wanted more federal programs to be cost-justified. The distinguishing features of the Reagan strategy were its comprehensiveness and its sophisticated public relations. According to Wright, "previous administrations' efforts at management improvement have met with varying degrees of success, but they have not generally continued as permanent, government-wide initiatives." The Reagan program aimed to bring about lasting change.

Detailed objectives were set forth, usually associated with specially created White House consulting teams such as the Task Force on Regulatory Relief, headed by Vice President Bush, and the Private Sector Survey on Cost Control, headed by J. Peter Grace.

Reagan's strict, businesslike priorities had an immediate and severe impact on federal information activities, which, in many instances, could not survive the cost-benefit analysis adopted by the administration. Accorded less emphasis as a public resource, information products were now expected to pay their way as commodities. As a consequence, many services previously supplied to the public at little or no cost soon had a fee attached or were abandoned entirely.

Reduction of Publications

In April 1981, Reagan imposed a moratorium on the production and procurement of new audiovisual aids and printed publications maintaining that the government was spending too much money on "public relations." The same month, the OMB issued a bulletin that required all agencies to review and reduce planned publications. The following fall, OMB Director David Stockman issued two memoranda requiring heads of departments to pay closer attention to "information centers" and to consider whether information functions could be provided just as efficiently by the private sector. Moreover, agencies were to submit separate requests for all existing publications to be continued after January 15, 1982.

The administration's information-cutting programs at the agency level moved on from there. Within eighteen months, the government announced that 2,000 publications and dozens of government depositories had been eliminated. Then and later, OMB officials maintained that only unnecessary materials had been affected. In 1982, Wright entertained the press on the subject by displaying a large wastepaper basket filled with some of the periodicals targeted for elimination. He singled out such publications as "Buying a Christmas Tree" and "Brassieres, Girdles and Allied Garments," an annual trade report from the Commerce Department, as examples of waste.

While a great many of the eliminated publications may have been superfluous, the government's claim that this was true of all of the defunct publications was disingenuous. Clearly, political considerations were involved. One example was the elimination of *The Car Book*, put out by the National Highway Transportation Safety Administration. This publication, which contained data on the crashworthiness of various makes of automobiles, sold 1.5 million copies. Millions of car accidents each year as well as the large number of auto recalls indicated a need for this publication. But *The Car Book* had made the auto industry mad and was therefore sent to the trash bin.

Another example of censorship of publications on political grounds was the Occupational Safety and Health Administration's attempted cancellation of a brochure explaining the dangers of cotton dust. The head of OSHA at that time, Thorne Auchter, considered the cover photo of the publication offensive because it showed a cotton dust worker who was suffering from brown lung disease. Auchter's decision to do away with the brochure was made after 50,000 copies had already been printed. He first tried to have the copies destroyed and then settled for replacing the cover.

Many publications that were not canceled were made much more costly. Agency bulletins, previously free, were given a price tag. Between January 1981 and June 1982, the price of the *Federal Register* rose from seventy-five to three hundred dollars during the same period that it shrank to a third of its original size. The large size of the *Register* had often been used by opponents of regulation as proof of how bureaucratic red tape had gotten out of hand. But the *Regis-*

ter is also an important source of information concerning the new and revised operations of government. All new regulations must be published in the *Register* when they are first introduced and again after a final decision has been reached. This process is both a valuable record of things that would otherwise go unnoticed and a mechanism for furthering the goal of openness in agency activities. The difficulties raised by the administration's failure to explain many of its actions are taken up again in the following chapters.

President Reagan entered office with plans to centralize his administration and exercise stricter control over government information-collection activities. With help from conservative think tanks, a strengthened OMB, and his own clear ideological views for domestic and foreign policy, the president swiftly carried out major elements of his program, including a drastic reduction in public access to information collected about business and the imposition of unprecedented restrictions on the behavior of government personnel. Many of these restrictions are contained in executive orders or are the result of a sweeping reorganization of the executive branch. The consequences of the Reagan policies, therefore, will last beyond the Reagan presidency unless modified by future presidents. Meantime, they pose a fundamental challenge to long-standing constitutional values in favor of free speech and public awareness about the activities of government.

Chapter 3

THE BUDGET AND BEYOND
The Office of
Management and Budget

IT BOILS DOWN TO A POLITICAL QUESTION,
NOT OF BUDGET POLICY OR ECONOMIC POL-
ICY, BUT WHETHER WE CAN CHANGE THE
HABITS OF THE POLITICAL SYSTEM.

—David Stockman, Director
Office of Management and Budget

Around the corner from the White House was the nerve center of the executive branch under Reagan—the Office of Management and Budget. In addition to drawing up the federal budget, this agency, headed by a zealous midwesterner named David Stockman, was in charge of federal information management, governmentwide protection of privacy, and oversight of most of the regulatory agencies. Expanding its powers greatly during the 1980's, the OMB assumed a position of authority unprecedented in the nation's history, rivaling that of the three traditional branches of government. Taken together, its budgetary and regulatory functions raised fundamental constitutional issues regarding centralization of political power.

35

ACCUMULATION OF POWER

The OMB started out in 1921 as the Bureau of the Budget, the agency responsible for assembling and coordinating the funding requirements of the federal government. Under Franklin Roosevelt, it was moved from the Treasury Department to the Office of the President. The Federal Reports Act of 1942 put the bureau in charge of clearing reports. Agencies were required to submit proposals for collecting data and were permitted to act upon only those activities that were not vetoed by the bureau. Later, in 1950, its responsibilities were again enlarged to include the coordination of statistical operations. From then on, it gradually assumed more and more of the powers of a central management authority, its rising status paralleling the steadily increasing role of American government. In the 1960's and 1970's, the government expanded to include more social and economic planning, public assistance programs, environmental regulation, and scientific research. A new kind of federal machine emerged, which dealt with political issues through regulatory channels and the budget process at least as much as they were addressed through the electoral process. The collection and exchange of information was often at the heart of this activity.

During this period, officials in the executive branch perceived a need for some kind of central agency that would oversee the rapidly growing activities of government. In 1970, following extensive examination of this issue, Congress renamed the Bureau of the Budget the Office of Management and Budget. Less than a decade later, the agency's role was again enlarged, as President Jimmy Carter sought to give the OMB an advisory role in decision making by agencies, partly to limit certain regulatory programs that had provoked strong criticism from industry. Carter's plan was still in rough form when Congress designated the OMB as the coordinator of a legislative initiative to stem the growth of federal paperwork and improve the quality of the information collected by the government. The Paperwork Reduction Act of 1980 was a turning point in the OMB's career. The act created a new Office of Information and Regulatory Affairs (OIRA) within the OMB, which was given primary responsibility for achieving the act's objectives. Its duties included improving management of information resources within the government, oversight of statistical policy, guiding implementation of the protection of privacy, and paperwork reduction. In addition, the scope of the report-clearance function that had been assigned to the OMB's predecessor agency in 1942 was expanded by the Paperwork Reduction Act, which put the regulatory agencies within the OMB's jurisdiction for the first time.

By the time Ronald Reagan was inaugurated in 1981, the OMB had already grown from its original role as the budget accountant into a manager of information. But the Reagan administration had even greater ambitions for it. The OMB was called upon to play a major role in the administration's plan to limit the scope of federal activities. Only two months into his term, the new president issued Executive Order 12291, which empowered the OMB to mold and supervise all of the operations of agencies of the executive branch.[1] The independent agencies, being directly responsible to Congress, were not covered by the order. However, the OMB was able to influence many of their programs through its power over the budget and agencywide collection of information.

The order placed the OMB firmly astride three of the administration's priorities: a balanced budget, deregulation, and reduction of paperwork. Its combined strengths were justified by administration officials as essential to the successful implementation of the president's programs. However, as the OMB proceeded to implement presidential policies—often doing so behind the scenes—it came into conflict with congressional objectives that had been written into the legislation that created the complex network of regulatory agencies. The basis of the OMB's authority to interfere with regulatory activities was unclear. Doubt about its legitimacy in the regulatory arena only increased owing to the fact that the OMB was less inclined than other agencies to document its actions and be open to scrutiny. Consequently, the OMB's activities were soon seen by many members of Congress and public groups as endangering the democratic process.

While the overall powers of the OMB raised serious questions, this chapter focuses on its information-related programs. Through curtailing, transferring, and redirecting the flow of information among government bodies and between the public and private sector, the OMB, under Reagan, was in a position to alter dramatically the rules and conditions for influencing government activity. Much of this was accomplished through the agency's role in the budget process and its attempt to supervise the regulatory agencies.

THE OFFICE OF MANAGEMENT AND BUDGET AND THE BUDGET PROCESS

The budget process is an elaborate series of thousands of overlapping negotiations renewed each year when the president announces his blueprint for the allocation of the nation's resources. From start to finish, the president's priorities are being tested, even as valuable information is being provided in regard to his views on foreign policy, regulation, taxation, and myriad other major issues.

After the Reagan administration took office, David Stockman was given a clear mandate to make sweeping budget cuts, leaving no agency unscathed. Even before introducing a new budget, he persuaded Congress to approve billions of dollars in deferrals and recisions from earlier years. The budget process of 1981 amounted to a political coup d'état for Reagan. Congress accepted severe across-the-board reductions and the elimination of many programs with scarcely a whimper. The economic crisis at that time was a primary reason for the strong austerity measures adopted. Not only deficits, however, but ideology was at stake. As the young budget general told the journalist William Greider, the budget was not just a question of numbers. "It boils down to a political question, not of budget policy or economic policy, but whether we can change the habits of the political system."[2]

Reduction of Paperwork

In each of Stockman's annual budgets, the reduction of paperwork was a principal goal. The OMB worked toward that goal by seeking to reduce the amount of time, measured in "burden hours," that companies and individuals were required to spend in filling out government forms. A principal objective of this process was to unburden large and small businesses so that they might embark on new projects and investments.[3]

Running parallel to the fiscal budget, one year behind to reflect program changes, was the Information Collection Budget developed by the OMB. It gave to each agency an annual allowance for collecting information in order to limit the costs to individuals, private organizations, and state and local government of filling out forms and records for the federal government. Each year as the budget was being prepared, agencies submitted descriptions of their record-keeping requirements, estimated in terms of burden hours. After approving or modifying these figures, the OMB assembled the comprehensive Information Collection Budget. That budget, in time, was reported to Congress as part of the OMB's report on the Paperwork Act, though veto power on the agencies' reports lay solely with the

OMB. In this way, the agencies' information activities could be trimmed, nearly always without public discussion or debate.

The OMB found the Information Collection Budget to be an effective management tool. Indeed, it was the primary source for the president's announcement in January, 1984, that "over 300 million hours of government required paperwork each year" had been eliminated.[4] Yet the significance of such an extraordinary figure should be evaluated in terms of content as well as size. In the same speech, Reagan reported a 25 percent reduction in federal regulation, without indicating which programs had been eliminated and whether deregulation left information gaps in important areas of public policy. In 1983, both the Highway Traffic Accident Report and Accident Investigation Reporting were eliminated. The OMB calculated that each of these steps saved 18 million burden hours. The issue that merits public investigation is whether the elimination of these forms reflected a declining commitment to transit safety. Moreover, 56 percent of federal paperwork is associated with peoples' obtaining federal benefits.[5] These payments include research and procurement contracts in addition to monies allocated to millions of citizens in Social Security, Medicaid, disability payments, and other assistance programs. Here, paperwork reduction potentially touches upon tangible and immediate human need. In general, the question becomes: Who, exactly, benefits from the rapid reduction of paperwork?

The OMB has used the budget process to provide agencies with incentives to consolidate or transfer out certain activities. Along with their annual estimates of burden hours attached to information programs, agencies were required to consider whether the same information programs could be performed as well or better by a private organization. In 1982, the president's budget blueprint for the next six years, "Reform 88," included plans for continuing big reductions in agency publications and stepping up efforts to transfer government information functions to the private sector.

Stockman planned to change government information programs through large-scale reorganization of agency departments and programs, although in at least two instances his schemes were thwarted. One example was the Department of Energy. While attempting to abolish the department, the administration proposed to transfer the Energy Information Administration to the Department of Commerce. Because the plan to abolish the Energy Department failed, the EIA remains within that department today, though it has become a pale version of its former self. Budgets for data analysis and information collection were slashed, affecting, among other things, forecast of energy supply and demand relied upon by industry. In addition, the OMB proposed to eliminate the Financial Reporting System, in which information was gathered on the financial structure of energy companies. The system was preserved only after Congress vetoed the proposal.

Similar episodes took place relative to information programs at other agencies, including the OMB itself. The OMB's lack of enthusiasm for significant federal information programs was starkly revealed in the lack of resources allocated to two of the OMB's own primary areas of responsibility—statistics and privacy.

Statistics

The gathering of statistics on many facets of American life has been accepted as a primary responsibility of the federal government throughout the history of the country; the requirement that the government carry out a decennial census was written into the Constitution itself. A statistical policy unit existed from 1933 to 1980, almost always under the auspices of the OMB and its predecessor agencies, and was responsible for overseeing the decentralized statistical gathering system of the federal government. The importance of statistical activity was underscored by two high-level studies carried out in the late 1970's, each of which recommended a strengthening of such functions through large increases in personnel and funding.[6]

Ignoring these recommendations, the OMB proceeded to abolish its statistical policy unit entirely and to downgrade statistical analysis amidst deregulation and paperwork reduction priorities. The number of OMB personnel working full-time on statistics fell from twenty-five to between three and five during the first three years of the administration. In 1982, the agency's statistical policy branch, which coordinated governmentwide data collection, was eliminated, and most of its congressionally mandated work was distributed, on a part-time basis, to desk officers who also reviewed agency programs for paperwork burden estimates and regulatory relief objectives. The dissolution of the focal point for statistical activity was opposed by many groups. Henry Reuss, chairman of the Joint Economic Committee of Congress, called this action "a further step backward for intelligent and informed policymaking and [it] will only confirm those who have dark fears of a massive statistical coverup in the making."

In May 1983, Stephen E. Feinberg, chairman of the Committee on National Statistics, National Research Council, before a Senate committee, called for "strong and effective coordination of federal statistics . . . to increase their relevance for national policy purposes, to protect their integrity, to improve their quality and to collect and use them more efficiently." He said, "Currently, the OMB is failing to provide effective coordination of federal statistics; in particular, it is not determining overall program priorities nor achieving an efficient, well-planned total program. The continued absence of effective coordination already has impaired the quality of the statistical program and threatens to have even more serious consequences."[7]

This decline in quality had become all too clear to companies and organizations that used federal statistics. As Katherine K. Wallman, director of the Council of Professional Associations on Federal Statistics, said, "Those who have worked within the government's statistical system . . . have long stressed the irony of the inverse relationship between the growth in the scope and importance of our federal statistical programs and the decline in resources allocated for planning, evaluating and improving the products of the federal statistical agencies. Within the past two years, this anomaly has moved from the realm of chronic weaknesses to the domain of acute problems."[8]

At congressional hearings held in March and June of 1982, the OMB was said to be indifferent to the importance of federal statistical collection and analysis. This criticism and the OMB's response revealed an important disagreement over the government's responsibility. Christopher DeMuth, an OMB official, defended the fact that his agency had subordinated statistical operations to deregulatory activities and paperwork reduction. Statistical activities, like all other programs, he stated, had to satisfy the same cost-benefit criteria. On another occasion, DeMuth told a reporter, "In the past, agencies collected much greater detail than was needed for national policymaking purposes. It is understood now that agencies justify their data collection programs to the OMB in terms of the needs of federal agencies alone, not of states, local governments or private firms for their own marketing purposes."

This approach was not acceptable to those concerned about the deterioration in statistical programs. A congressional subcommittee report published in 1982 congratulated the OMB on its success in eliminating paperwork yet concluded that the agency had virtually ignored all other aspects of the Paperwork Reduction Act. In particular, the act was intended to improve the *accuracy* of government data. The OMB had failed to ensure that important information continued to be analyzed even while the objectives of paperwork reduction and deregulation of business were being pursued.

The charge that the OMB had ignored many of the areas it had been charged to direct was repeated in April 1983 in a report prepared at the request of the chairman of the House Committee on Government Operations. In that report, the comptroller general of the General Accounting Office concluded that since the Paperwork Reduction Act was enacted, "long-range planning activities have not been completed; statistical policy directives have not been reissued; no evaluations of statistical programs have been performed; resources applied to the OMB's statistical policy coordination and oversight responsibilities have diminished sharply."[9]

The fact that the OMB had failed to make a separate assessment of the importance of federal statistics was a key factor in its allowing statistical policy to be downgraded. Unfortunately, quality in statistical measurement is not easily regained. Expertise, when lost, may take years to replace, while key data may be lost forever.

Privacy

Another area where the OMB set standards for government information activity was the protection of privacy. The Privacy Act of 1974 put the OMB in charge of monitoring the compliance of agencies with the law, which was designed to offer protection for individual privacy through rules of nondisclosure and procedures for prior notification of and file correction by affected persons. The OMB was to gather information on compliance with the Privacy Act and issue rules to keep protection of privacy up to date with technology.

The OMB devoted only limited resources and attention to this important area. Since 1981, few new privacy regulations were issued, and no additional personnel were assigned to this function. Furthermore, the OMB actively supported administration initiatives that posed serious threats to privacy. Many of these actions centered on increased sharing of computerized information about individuals among government agencies. This practice, called computer matching, expanded significantly after the OMB weakened relevant restrictions in 1981. Ostensibly to fight fraud, the names of recipients of public assistance were matched against federal payrolls. In addition, the Social Security Administration gave what was supposed to be confidential information on the whereabouts of thousands of people to the Selective Service, which was trying to locate young men who had failed to register for the draft. While the OMB often was not the source of such blatant incursions on privacy, it was ultimately responsible for the damage inflicted. John Shattuck, legislative director of the American Civil Liberties Union, speaking about the alarming erosion of the individual's right to privacy that has occurred under Reagan, said OMB inaction and misinterpretation were bringing about a "vanishing right of privacy" that would take years to undo, if ever.

Perhaps the most disturbing aspects of this trend were the rationales offered by the OMB, the Justice Department, and other offices to defend government abuse of privacy. The needs of the federal bureaucracy to collect on its loans and to monitor peaceful dissent were placed ahead of basic constitutional rights. An administration that had come into office promising to get government off the backs of the people was more than ever looking over their shoulders.

The national budget process and the Information Collection Budget were two of the main ways that the OMB brought about important changes in information policy. Its control over the fiscal budget could be checked to some extent by Congress. However, because much of the office's plans were passed along simply as numbers, Congress was not privy to the office's exhaustive agency reviews or lists of what was being eliminated. Also, Congress usually was not in a position to judge the information-related costs of programs that were downgraded by the OMB. Under Reagan, budget reductions resulted in the elimination of thousands of publications and scores of agency jobs and government programs related to information. In each instance, the cuts could be justified on the grounds of fiscal austerity. Competing values and objectives were not raised, particularly when information programs had to vie for congressional attention with life and death issues such as Social Security and defense. As Ralph Nader has stated, information policies were more vulnerable than many other areas because they generally lacked an organized constituency.[10] In addition, Congress had no authority over the Information Collection Budget.

THE OFFICE OF MANAGEMENT AND BUDGET AND THE REGULATORY AGENCIES

The OMB's supervision of regulatory programs in the 1980's had a profound impact on government information policies, ranging from public access to information concerning the environment to agency responses to requests under the Freedom of Information Act. The aggressive role assigned to the OMB by Ronald Reagan rested upon a belief that most agency departments should be centrally managed. This was hardly an orginal idea. In the Nixon years, a special Advisory Council, headed by Roy Ash and composed largely of top-level corporate executives, made recommendations for institutionalizing budget and program evaluation, legislative clearance, and personnel decisions within one office. These suggestions were the basis of the lengthy congressional deliberations that resulted in the creation of the new management and budget office.

Not long after it came into existence, the OMB's credibility as a professional and politically neutral management body became tainted. When much of the Nixon staff became preoccupied with defending themselves against Watergate allegations, the OMB moved in to fill the policy-making void. During congressional oversight hearings in 1973, Rep. J. J. Pickle declared that the OMB had become "the invisible government of the United States" and might be "unintentionally threatening our constitutional concept of public government." In response to these charges, the powers of the OMB were curtailed in the Gerald Ford administration.

Jimmy Carter sought to bring the OMB back to a role of managerial importance but faced strong opposition from some of his own agency heads. Carter's efforts were brought to fruition only after he was out of office. In several ways, Carter set the stage for his successor. Indeed, he is often given credit for the initial impetus for Reagan's war on the bureaucracy. Carter outlined important elements of future OMB activity, including oversight of new agency regulations. Also, the OMB's powers grew directly on account of the Paperwork Reduction Act, important elements of which were pursued by officials in the Carter administration. Furthermore, it was in part in reaction to the indecisiveness that afflicted the later Carter years that Congress was initially so willing to accept Reagan's blueprints for deregulation and centralization of the executive branch. These plans were first outlined in an executive order that, to this day, is of uncertain legitimacy as a source of major government authority.

Evaluation of Agency Regulations

Executive Order 12291 put the OMB in charge of evaluating all new and existing government regulations according to cost-benefit criteria that were to be developed by the

OMB. Agency proposals had to be submitted to the OMB before their publication in the *Federal Register.* Further, the OMB's role in all rule making continued throughout the process and included final approval of agency action. No conditions were set down with regard to OMB record keeping or compliance with the Administrative Procedure Act, a procedural law enacted to ensure openness and accountability in agency functions.

The profound impact that this change in procedure had on Washington has been widely noted. A report from the Congressional Research Service concluded that the OMB's new powers effectively undermined congressional statutes—the only legal basis of agency action.[11] Susan and Martin Tolchin, in their book *Dismantling America,* described how OMB intervention "created a new regulatory landscape, a still life actually, with the presidential agencies fearful of issuing new regulations."[12] The OMB also brought about a dramatic change in the exchange of information between numerous agencies and public groups and, in addition, subverted congressional access to agency-held information.

According to Shannon Ferguson, head of OMB Watch, a nonprofit group that was formed in 1982 to monitor the offices's actions, the OMB has actively blocked public access to information about activities of the executive branch.[13] Ferguson's complaint was also raised during congressional hearings on the toxic waste program of the Environmental Protection Agency. The OMB was accused of withholding essential information and of meeting secretly with industry representatives. The OMB resisted Congress's requests for information up until the time when this inquiry threatened to become a major national scandal.

More than once, the OMB was charged with making contact with industry groups that it favored and imposing their interests directly on agency chiefs. Such communication often took place by telephone, and few written records were kept. Charges were brought of corruption and usurpation of agency authority. The OMB was upheld in court regarding its contacts with outsiders, but it was told to make written records of information that was relevant to any proceeding it sought to influence. One problem caused by the OMB's refusal to keep many records was the difficulty encountered in attempts to locate the officials responsible for changes in agency policies. Certain of the OMB's goals were in line with those of the agency officials appointed by the president, but not always. In the latter instances, the OMB's efforts to impose its will undermined the system of accountability that relies on written records to explain final decisions and made appeal of those decisions more strenuous.

Other Limitations on Agencies

Apart from influencing rule making by agencies, the OMB limited their information activities in other ways. Printed forms that were essential elements of regulations were vetoed. In the fall of 1981, for example, the OMB vetoed Federal Communications Commission forms that collected data on affirmative-action programs of broadcast licensees. In that instance, word got out to the public and the move was blocked. In other instances, there was no such public notification. In addition, agency information collection allowances were severely restricted, forcing agencies to eliminate research, education programs, and other activities. In a short period of time, the very character of agencies involved in social programs changed from supplying the public with information to preventing its release. The word from the top seemed to be: Withhold unless required by law to do otherwise.

The OMB imposed information restrictions also by issuing regulations of its own, called circulars. Some shifted information activities to the private sector; others called for large reductions in periodicals and audiovisual material or aimed at restricting information that could be shared by government contractors.

In the spring of 1983, the OMB's dim view of public participation in politics was written into circular A-122. The agency proposed to forbid government funding for groups that used any part of government equipment, facilities, or personnel for political advocacy. For many years, Congress had enacted laws that required that organizations keep separate account of money from the government for projects and money from other sources used for political lobbying. The basis of these rules was that taxpayer funds should not be used to advance political objectives. Under the OMB's proposed rule, however, government contractors and nonprofit groups were to be asked to choose between government funding and legitimate public outreach.

The OMB's proposal created an immediate nationwide uproar, unifying such diverse groups as the U.S. Chamber of Commerce, the American Lung Association, and the Disabled Veterans of America. In hearings held in the spring and fall of 1983, the latter groups, following the OMB revision of its proposal, testified on the devastating effect this rule would have. Evan Kemp, executive director of the Disability Rights Center, said the rule would reverse most of the progress disabled persons had made in gaining the attention of lawmakers. These groups, he stated, simply had to continue speaking out in order not to be forgotten. Robert Thompson, head of the U.S. Chamber of Commerce, opposed the rule on the grounds that it was "unnecessary and unworkable" and would violate constitutional freedoms of expression and petition.[14]

The OMB's revised proposal would have allowed groups to make contact with officials of the executive branch but not elected representatives. OMB officials explained this discrepancy in terms of the need of certain interests to have access to administration agencies to conduct business. Rep.

Jack Brooks, one of those who led the opposition in Congress to circular A-122, took issue with this reasoning, saying that public access to members of Congress was at least as important as access to the executive branch. "I am particularly concerned by the provisions of this proposal that appear to interfere with the flow of essential information to Congress and other legislative bodies," Brooks stated.

USES OF POWER

The issues in need of further deliberation involve not the OMB's essential function but, rather, the ways in which it has used or twisted its authority. Congress delegated a great deal of authority to the OMB to give it the leverage Congress deemed necessary to coordinate federal activities and minimize waste and inefficiency. Congress did not, however, intend to erect a superagency. It did not give the OMB authority to supplant agency decisions or change the regulatory process from one of openness to one of private conversations.

Furthermore, Congress has long recognized that the visibility of governmental actions and the accountability of those who perform them can do much to preserve public participation in government. Accordingly, it passed laws such as the Freedom of Information Act and the Administrative Procedure Act. It deliberately decentralized its regulatory agencies in order to prevent corruption and encourage active sharing of information between administrative agencies and the public.

In 1981, the OMB took the power it had received from Congress to oversee the budget, paperwork, statistics, privacy, and the complex web of regulatory information and carried it much further. It overrode agency decisions and narrowed the regulatory process to a series of private conversations. It dramatically increased threats to privacy through its own guidelines for disclosure and retention of information. It directed its budget power to strict ideological ends. It devalued the objective of public participation in government in the name of efficiency and deregulation. Indifferent to the need for widespread dissemination of information about government, fond of meeting behind closed doors, and concerned almost exclusively with the interests of large corporations, the OMB used its vast powers to seal government off from many sectors of society that had come to view government as an effective, and perhaps the only, means of protecting their needs. Congress had not anticipated these results, yet also it did not act quickly enough to control the OMB's endeavors.

The consequences of negative policies toward the availability of information can be as swift as they are hard to measure. This is another reason for vigilant and ongoing consideration of government information priorities that need to be incorporated into government programs. The day that separate assessments are made and standards are set to guide the enforcement of information policies will be the day the OMB is once again brought to heel as merely a subsidiary agency of the executive branch.

Chapter 4

DRAWING THE BLINDS
The Regulatory Agencies

THIS IS THE MOST CLOSED GOVERNMENT SINCE THE FOUNDING OF THE AMERICAN REPUBLIC AND NO ONE KNOWS IT. WE'RE TALKING ABOUT INFORMATION, THE MOST IMPORTANT GOVERNMENT SERVICE.
—Sheldon Samuels, Director of Health and Safety/AFL-CIO Industrial Union Department

In recent years, the voluminous form-filing and record-keeping requirements of federal agencies have given rise to a chorus of complaints from business, local governments, and private citizens. Objections range from the corporate lament that paperwork detracts from more productive pursuits to charges brought by groups and individuals of government meddling and serious invasions of privacy. However valid some of these objections, what goes under the name of paperwork is often the collection of vital information. What is annoying paperwork to a corporation may be the only way in which the public and the federal government itself can learn about activities of business in vital areas of public policy.

More generally, information activities are an integral part

of the overall operations of most regulatory agencies. Included in these activities are research, regulatory announcements, telephone contacts, and protection of privacy.

Concern over excessive government paperwork did not appear for the first time in the 1970's. Thirty years earlier, Congress had established limits in this area in the Federal Reports Act of 1942. The law stated that information needed by federal agencies was to be obtained with "a minimum burden upon business enterprises." In addition, the information collected was to be held as short a time as possible in order to minimize incursions of privacy and was to avoid unnecessary duplication. As government expanded its role in the economy, following World War II, inevitably it required more information about many facets of economic activity. A substantial increase in paperwork was not good or evil but unavoidable.

Later, in response to calls for government action in new areas of social as well as economic concern, including the environment, health care, and product safety, major pieces of legislation were enacted in the 1960's and 1970's. Many of these included explicit charges to the agencies they created to gather voluminous data, to share information with experts and others, and to embark on extensive research programs. For example, the Clean Air Act amendments of 1970 instructed officials of the Environmental Protection Agency (EPA) to collect and disseminate data on chemical and physical causes of air pollution.[1]

The regulatory process set forth in most areas of social regulation was a participatory one. Individuals and citizen organizations were expected to play a significant role in agency deliberations by submitting comments on proposed regulations and alerting officials to problems. The underlying law governing all agency activities, the Administrative Procedure Act, bound agencies to notify the public of new areas of regulatory action, to conduct proceedings openly, and to allow sufficient time for public contributions. In the new regulatory laws of the 1970's, special provisions carried the emphasis on public involvement into areas such as public education, access to records of work-place injuries kept by corporations, and training of local citizens for inspections of the environment.

Within the space of ten years, a new framework emerged in which federal government officials had closer contact with more elements of society and many more people had direct access to the regulatory process. Issues of intense public concern, including the death of tens of thousands of workers each year as a result of hazardous equipment and exposure to dangerous chemicals, could only be addressed if massive efforts were undertaken to research the causes, effects, and means of preventing these problems. And so the channels of communication widened as never before.

Along with these new activities, there was a proliferation of agency forms, record-keeping requirements, and other types of paperwork. Some of this increase was recognized within the government as unnecessary or superfluous. Furthermore, many companies found fault with the rising tide of paperwork on the grounds that it was not only wasteful of the government's resources but inhibited their own productivity. Responding to these concerns, Congress created, in 1974, a Commission on Federal Paperwork under the direction of the OMB. Interestingly, in the course of carrying out its mandate to recommend ways of limiting paperwork, the commission generated a lot of paper of its own. By the time it completed its work, it had published 36 reports and 649 official recommendations.[2]

In its first report to Congress (1978) on the results of the commission's work, the OMB took a broad approach to the paperwork problem, looking at the many reasons—rational or not—for the widespread resentment at the extent of filing federal forms and other paperwork activities. Admitting that there existed serious questions of redundancy and inefficiency, the report maintained that because most paperwork served essential purposes directly tied to regulatory objectives, only so much could be eliminated and even that would require careful consideration of the trade-offs involved. The report indicated that paperwork should be evaluated in light of the *two* objectives set forth by the Carter administration: making the regulatory process more efficient and making it easier for the public to understand and participate in the work of the federal agencies.[3] A direct result of the latter was a presidential order, signed in March 1978, requiring agencies to write regulations in plain English.[4]

Three years later, the Reagan administration began operations with a different view of the need to streamline federal paperwork. As occurred with the OMB's expansion, the approach employed by Reagan to attack the paperwork problem relied very much on plans and research developed in the previous administration, but it had stricter policy objectives. A central goal of the Reagan presidency was deregulation. Gone was talk of needing to balance the regulatory agencies' need for information or the value of public input against the goal of reducing paperwork. In the new administration, officials from the president on down to agency clerks committed themselves to ensuring that the government imposed the minimum reporting requirements on the private sector.

To this end, agency chiefs were appointed who were opposed to the "public interest" goals of their own agencies and were committed to cost-benefit analysis. Interestingly, not one of these officials seemed to realize that information collection might help in such analysis. The publications, reports, press releases, and other materials that had served to involve the wider public in agency activities were soon drastically reduced. Agency forms were consolidated and eliminated to the extent permissible. Each year, Congress was urged to get rid of the thousands of information provisions contained in legislation.

Arthur Amolsch, head of the public affairs office at the Federal Trade Commission between 1973 and 1976, later coeditor and publisher of *FTC Watch,* a newsletter on the agency's activities, saw few similarities between the office he once ran and that run by Tom Fakar, his successor under Reagan. "In the past," Amolsch said, "you could call and ask about a program, talk about an injury or anything under our jurisdiction, and if the person on the phone couldn't answer the question, he'd get someone who could call you back pronto. These days, people there have no hesitation about saying 'I don't know,' and leaving it at that, unless you're from one of their corporate clients. Also, they don't like giving out information they've got. They delay publications, or print way too few. The consequences of such practices, of course, is that there are many fewer people calling these days, whether they be private individuals or local governments."[5]

As a result of the attitude within the administration that information should either not be collected in the first place or else not be shared, except with the beneficiaries of deregulation, across the executive branch and several independent agencies the link with the public was severed. There was an astonishing array of cutbacks in research and educational activities. For example, during the first two years of the Reagan administration, the staff of the National Highway Transportation and Safety Administration (NHTSA) was cut by 30 percent, mainly in the areas of technical research, public affairs, and publications. This reduction ensured that there would be less information available to the public concerning dangerous vehicles and auto emissions. Carol McKenna, a research scientist who has been at the agency since the mid 1970's, attributed much of the changed character of the NHTSA to the absence of an agency head who was willing to resist budgetary austerity. "Joan Claybrook, head of NHTSA under Carter, consistently fought the OMB's attempts to impose budget cutbacks," she said. "The present head of the Department of Transportation (which NHTSA is a part of) is all for that. As a consequence, NHTSA is a very different agency. There are many fewer people to deal with what concerns ordinary people. Many of the public-oriented people are gone."[6]

Federal agencies have different ways of fulfilling their basic responsibilities. For some, on-site investigations, backed up by monitoring at regional offices and decentralized educational programs, are the only effective means. Others, including those involved in dispersing payments, operate principally from Washington. For nearly all, during the first two years of the Reagan administration, there were many changes in their rules and procedures. According to the Administrative Procedure Act, the public should be notified about even minor changes in regulations through the *Federal Register*. Since there were a great many changes under Reagan, there should have been many more notices in the *Register*. Instead, the administration frequently boasted about having reduced the *Register*'s size by one third.

Not only were notices not placed in the *Register* to announce changes in programs, but agencies also circumvented the established procedures for implementing or amending major regulations. By law, agencies are required to issue printed notices prior to rule changes, inviting public comment, and again later to explain the adoption of final rules. In the 1980's, final rules were issued with announcements that no comment was necessary. So-called interim final rules were publicized, followed by a comment period that was far less meaningful than if comments had been received prior to the start of a new proceeding. At some agencies, public comment was discouraged through shortened deadlines for comments, while other agencies, such as the Federal Communications Commission and the Department of Health and Human Services, took to issuing several important notices at one time, as well as setting comment dates that were shorter than usual. Disregard for public participation was sometimes expressed summarily by the suspension or postponement of a rule with no notice whatsoever.

In sum, many tricks were employed in attempts to impede public participation in, and access to, agency information. The consequenes of the closed-door operations of the government went far beyond Washington, posing serious obstacles to local participation. Without government materials or interest, it was much harder for the public to remain well informed and to elicit the cooperation of industry employees, who felt freer to ignore public requests for records or other information.[7] The following sections provide selected examples of information restrictions at four federal agencies under Reagan.

DEPARTMENT OF HEALTH AND HUMAN SERVICES

The Department of Health and Human Services (HHS) is the agency most deeply involved in providing services to individuals and local governments. Included under its umbrella are Social Security, Aid to Families with Dependent Children (AFDC), Medicare, public health, disease control, and food and drug regulation. Nearly all Americans are in some way affected by the policies of this agency.

According to figures released by the OMB, after the Department of Agriculture, HHS was the department where the biggest paperwork reductions took place during the Reagan administration. This fact is a reliable indicator, not only of drastic reductions in HHS budget appropriations, but of the extent to which the public was not kept informed.

The HHS issued many fewer press releases, rule-making notices, and informational bulletins. Valuable data concerning many programs, which were relied upon by local health-care, social-work, and educational professionals were withheld or no longer collected. The *Annual Survey of Child Nutrition* as well as the *Annual Immunization Survey* were not published between 1980 and 1983, though the information was still collected.

Drastic budget cutbacks meant that the offices most in contact with the public had fewer people to answer questions. According to Paul Smith, this was one of the biggest problems at the HHS. The information network that sustained the delivery of hundreds of vital services was thereby endangered.

Representatives of nonprofit organizations affected by the HHS disagreed as to whether the agency had deliberately set about crippling information programs or had simply overlooked this area in its plan to shrink the size of the agency. Even if an agency's failure to provide notification was unintentional, however, the consequences of its actions were nonetheless cruel. On several occasions, the HHS neglected to provide critical information to the recipients of its benefit programs. Not being adequately informed of changes, many AFDC and Supplemental Security Income (SSI) recipients found themselves disqualified and unsure of how to appeal.

Another example whereby the HHS showed a startling insensitivity to the value of public comment on a matter of great importance concerned the so-called Katie Beckett ruling. Regulations were formulated as a response to the problem of certain child recipients of SSI payments who remained in institutions because going home would have meant that the parents' income would have been attributed to them, thereby disqualifying them from receiving Medicaid benefits. To have them remain in an institution, therefore, presented less of a financial burden to a lower-income family. This situation became a public issue in the spring of 1981. President Reagan highlighted the problem during a press conference, during which he spoke of Katie Beckett, a disabled child. However, rather than addressing the problem by inviting public comment and attempting to formulate a solution that would serve the tens of thousands of Katie Becketts around the country, the HHS issued an "interim final rule" allowing states to apply for more funds on a case-by-case basis. This ad hoc reform meant there would be long delays before the vast majority of affected children could return home. To make matters even worse, when Congress adopted its own solution, which allowed states to create Medicaid entitlements for children like Katie Beckett, the HHS responded to this rebuke by making little effort to announce this important change.

In the course of more than three years, the HHS pulled back from providing services in the form of reports, advice, and information that affected the lives of millions of individuals. Being at the receiving end of government programs has rarely been easy or comfortable. Nonetheless, in the past, the need for many of the programs administered by the HHS generally led the agency, at a minimum, to cooperate with local governmental and nonprofit agencies. This situation changed during the 1980's. The few examples provided here are but a small fraction of HHS actions that revealed its high level of indifference to, and ignorance of, the need for its services.

DEPARTMENT OF LABOR

Among the duties of the Department of Labor is that of seeing that working conditions throughout the nation are as safe and healthy as possible. When Congress passed the Mine Safety and Health Act and the Occupational Safety and Health Act in 1970, it established agencies within the

Department of Labor to set work-place health and safety standards, to enforce those standards in a way that assures protection for all workers, and to embark on a systematic research to assess undocumented health risks. In this area of regulation, beyond all others, education and training are essential.

According to Dr. Lauren Kerr, director of health and safety for the United Mine Workers Union of America, "There is one way to prevent occupational diseases: workers must know what they're exposed to and how to protect themselves. There are five million workplaces in this country and 15,000 of them employ 500 or more workers. That means 99% have less than 500 and 85% have less than 25 workers. The government will never have enough money to inspect all those places, nor would that be a wise expenditure of money. Workers have to have knowledge of what they're exposed to and how to protect themselves."[8]

Nonetheless, during every year of the Reagan administration, the Mine Health and Safety Administration's budget for worker education and enforcement generally was reduced significantly. The administration proposed cutbacks in the area of research totaling 40 percent. Under an earlier administration, the agency had set up nine regional centers, which trained company personnel and certified company programs in worker education. One of Reagan's first moves was to shut down these centers. In addition, numerous labeling standards proposed in the late 1970's were postponed or withdrawn completely. This type of regulation, no doubt, was in direct conflict with the philosophy of a conservative administration that looked to voluntary, nongovernmental solutions to social problems.

Many similar cutbacks took place at the Occupational Health and Safety Administration. Particularly hard hit by budget reductions was the New Directions grant program under which nongovernmental organizations such as rank and file Committees on Occupational Safety and Health

(COSH) were given money to inform workers and the general public about work-place hazards.

Several government booklets and films used to educate workers about health hazards were banned. One of these was on brown lung disease. As mentioned in chapter 2, the cover of a publication published by OSHA showed a worker who was suffering from the illness after working many years in cotton mills. In banning the book, former OSHA Director Thorne Auchter said that the cover photo "makes a dramatic statement that clearly establishes a biased viewpoint in the cotton dust issue." As a result of widespread public objection, the booklets were reissued but with a plain cover.

In October 1981, Auchter adopted a policy of making general safety inspections only for businesses whose lost days resulting from injury exceeded national averages. By law, companies must maintain logs of every recordable injury their workers suffer. By creating this exemption, Auchter provided an incentive for companies to neglect to record injuries, giving a false impression that their work places were safe, and removed the threat of inspection that helps make companies safety-conscious.

On another occasion, one of the very few safety regulations adopted by the agency during this period was immediately challenged on the grounds that it weakened state and local standards that had been adopted following intensive campaigns by COSH groups around the country. After resisting the nationwide move for laws guaranteeing workers' access to information about toxic substances, OSHA, in the fall of 1983, adopted right-to-know regulation that required manufacturers to label hazardous chemicals. The rule specified that any state laws were thereby preempted. In response, three states filed suit in federal court, charging that OSHA was trying to undermine laws in sixteen states that were stronger than the rule adopted by the agency. The federal regulation, they charged, covered fewer substances and would not protect workers in agriculture, construction, and service industries.

In January 1983, OSHA postponed for the second time a Carter administration proposal requiring the government to publish a list of suspected cancer-causing substances in the work place. The indefinite stay was widely criticized as weakening federal policy toward control of cancer.

Sheldon Samuels, director of health and safety for the American Federation of Labor-Congress of Industrial Organization's (AFL-CIO) industrial union department, maintained that "this is the most closed government since the founding of the American Republic and no one knows it. We're talking about information, the most important government service. Take trade secrets, industry convinces OMB or OSHA that a substance is a trade secret and can't be disclosed. I ask for an official decision on whether something is a trade secret and I'm told there is no one there to look into it. OSHA hasn't just reduced their staff, they've just cut off major functions of government."[9]

This position was also adopted in congressional testimony by representatives of some of the dozens of organizations concerned about the deterioration in government protection. Eula Bingham, former head of OSHA, who was widely considered to have been its most forceful administrator, informed the House Government Affairs Committee in 1983 that OSHA's scarce resources had been almost exclusively devoted to relaxing existing health standards. One way this was carried out was through sending signals to employers that they were free to ignore safety regulations.[10]

Nothing is more important to steady progress in the area of work-place safety than consistent reporting and research of hazardous conditions and resulting injuries. Nevertheless, this desired flow of information back and forth between the agencies responsible for improving conditions in the work place and among workers exposed to life-threatening conditions has been blocked in recent years.

Consequently, progress in this important area has been delayed. Potential solutions have been postponed indefinitely owing to agency indifference, while more and more lives are endangered by actions that thwart self-help and education at the local level.

THE ENVIRONMENTAL PROTECTION AGENCY

In few areas of regulation is information as powerful as it is in relation to environmental protection. The basic element of the Environmental Protection Agency's responsibility to clean up the nation's air and water, toxic landfills, and otherwise damaged natural resources is research. Nonetheless, from its beginning in 1970, the EPA's search for the causes and effects of environmental hazards has been vigorously opposed by industry in the contest between commerce and nature.

In 1981, a new EPA administrator was appointed, who sided with industry. During Anne Burford's tenure, all of the agency's programs were steadily weakened, including research and investigations. Few new rules were adopted. More than for other agencies, Congress included specific deadlines for the implementation of EPA projects in the underlying legislation. Nevertheless, in 1983, a Congressional Research Service study found that only 12 of 170 regulations relating to clean air, safe drinking water, noise, pesticides, radiation, solid waste, and clean water coincided with the EPA's January 1981 regulatory agenda.[11] The agency's attempts to deceive Congress about its inaction and industry connections in some of these areas is taken up in the next chapter dealing with the exchange of information between the executive branch and Congress in the early 1980's.

In addition, the agency often tried to keep from the public information concerning deteriorating environmental conditions and the EPA's lax enforcement of regulations. Since many poisonous substances are invisible or barely visible, one of the key informational tasks of the EPA is to publicize newly discovered hazards as soon as possible. During the Reagan administration, however, the EPA compiled and shared little, if any, new information that did not surface on account of flagrantly dangerous conditions such as occurred in dioxin-contaminated Times Beach, Missouri. Moreover, it often made statements or issued rules that falsely underestimated known environmental risks and injuries resulting from lax enforcement of regulations. In 1981, an agency rule prohibiting the disposal of containerized liquid wastes in landfills that lacked adequate safeguards was suspended. This action came not long after the discovery that toxic substances had permeated the land in Love Canal in upstate New York, requiring the evacuation of hundreds of families, and it was immediately blocked by environmental groups.

The EPA also moved to weaken standards on auto emissions, noise levels, and lead content in gasoline. Often these serious actions were taken quietly, through delayed initiation of rules that had been adopted in the late stages of the Carter administration or through amendments to regulations accomplished without public notice or opportunity for public comment.

The potential cost to human life augured by these actions was, of course, inestimable. The agency expended little effort, however, researching this issue. Particularly in the first two years, most "cost" data offered by Burford's EPA in its cost-benefit analyses of regulation pertained to ways in which environmental regulations burdened various industries. Fran Dubrowski, a veteran environmental attorney at the Natural Resources Defense Council, testified before Congress in 1983 on the agency's failure to enforce clean air regulations. Noting that the EPA had accorded little significance to the benefits of regulation to human health, she pointed out that the EPA tried to preclude this issue by slashing its own budget, while stating publicly that time and data constraints prevented detailed analyses of social-cost considerations.[12]

Another way in which the EPA deprived the public of valuable information was by altering record-keeping requirements for various industries, including ones required by law.

According to legislation passed in 1980 to galvanize resources for improving toxic conditions, companies that generated large amounts of hazardous substances were required to prepare three reports each year: an annual report, a yearly groundwater assessment survey, and a quarterly monitoring report. The regulations implementing this law were published in 1980; however, the first reports were not due until November 1981. Though these records were part of emergency relief, Burford approved an extension of the initial deadlines for all three reports, without notifying the public. When questioned, the EPA claimed the delays were justified because of the agency's plan to modify the rules so that they would apply to fewer companies. Public comment on this matter was not deemed essential.

Faced with pro-industry regulators, environmentalists frequently resorted to litigation or threats thereof and relied on the Freedom of Information Act to acquire material that might, in earlier times, have become available through regulatory proceedings or company records submitted to the agency. On many occasions, first requests under the FOIA were routinely denied and the denials later reversed on appeal.

Public support for environmental regulation in each of the areas covered by the EPA has been demonstrated in a steady series of reports and national surveys since the early 1970's. The need for information on the part of public groups, local governments, medical researchers, and others is clear. Hence, the EPA's failure to protect the public through research and investigations and its resistance to public attempts to gather information can be regarded as a national disgrace.

THE FEDERAL COMMUNICATIONS COMMISSION

The Federal Communications Commission regulates nationwide communications, be it by wire, broadcasting, cable, or satellite. In comparison with the HHS and other agencies that maintain direct contact with millions of people and hundreds of organizations through forms and publications, the FCC's licensing and monitoring of communications activity necessitate relatively little exchange of information. Throughout the investigations of the 1970's, the FCC was never mentioned in the list of agencies where excessive paperwork needed to be eliminated. Yet during the Reagan administration, the FCC distinguished itself by attaining one of the largest percent reductions in paperwork of all the regulatory agencies (see table).

The FCC chairman appointed by Reagan, Mark S. Fowler, was a dedicated deregulator. Fond of declaring his belief that the FCC had gone wrong back in the 1930's by tying itself to something as ridiculous as the public-interest standard of the 1934 Communications Act, Fowler aimed to eliminate as many rules and regulations as possible. His was, no doubt, an easier task than slashing benefit programs. The deregulation of communications could be accomplished without depriving people of food and shelter or endangering their health.

The commission's record in this period was one of steadily modifying and eliminating regulations so that information concerning the industry no longer reached the commission on a regular basis; at the same time it made it more difficult for public concerns to be heard. The Communications Act obligated the commission to monitor the perform-

PAPERWORK REDUCTION FROM THE FY 1980 BASE, FY 1982
(IN MILLIONS OF RESPONDENT HOURS)

Agency	FY 1980 Base	FY '80–82 Reduction	Percent Change from FY 1980
Total Government	1,477.0	−246.2	−16.7
Excluding Treasury	826.5	−187.6	−22.7
Departments:			
Agriculture	114.0	−23.5	−20.6
Commerce...........................	38.3	−36.1	−94.3
Defense	8.0	−1.7	−21.7
Education	9.0	−1.9	−21.1
Energy	17.9	−6.4	−36.0
Health and Human Services..............	83.8	−21.5	−25.6
Housing and Urban Development.........	21.5	−4.4	−20.4
Interior..............................	10.1	−2.0	−19.4
Justice	3.8	−0.7	−17.3
Labor	20.8	−5.2	−25.1
State................................	3.0	−0.4	−13.5
Transportation	271.0	−26.3	−9.7
Treasury.............................	650.5	−58.5	−9.0
Internal Revenue Service	(641.2)	(−57.7)	(−9.0)
Agencies:			
Civil Aeronautics Board	0.6	−0.1	−19.9
Commodity Futures Trading Comm.......	2.6	−0.3	−10.9
Consumer Product Safety Comm			−7.8
Environmental Protection Agency	8.4	−2.9	−35.1
Equal Employment Opportunity Comm ...	2.1	−0.6	−30.2
→ Federal Communications Comm..........	27.2	−17.4	−63.9
Federal Deposit Insurance Corp	1.5	−0.2	−15.0
Federal Emergency Management Agency..	0.5	−0.1	−15.0
Federal Home Loan Bank Board	9.7	−1.7	−17.6
Federal Reserve Board	6.9	−1.0	−15.1
Federal Trade Comm...................	0.2	−0.1	−30.1
General Services Admin.................	0.4		−3.3
Interstate Commerce Comm	2.1	−1.1	−55.0
National Aeronautics and Space Admin.	0.3	−0.1	−21.3
National Credit Union Admin	77.5	−15.3	−19.7
National Science Foundation.............	1.2	−0.1	−12.1
Nuclear Regulatory Comm...............	19.3	−9.4	−49.2
Office of Personnel Management..........	3.1	−0.3	−8.5
Railroad Retirement Board...............	0.6	−0.1	−18.8
Securities and Exchange Comm	46.8	−4.8	−10.3
Small Business Admin...................	0.8	−0.7	−16.0
Veterans Admin	6.4	−1.0	−16.0

Managing Federal Information Resources,
First Annual Report under the Paperwork Reduction Act of 1980,
Office of Management and Budget, April 1, 1982.

ance of radio and television stations to see that they were responsive to vital community needs and interests. In the two decades prior to the Fowler FCC, the agency had received a great deal of public information regarding ways in which their local stations were unresponsive. Public groups successfully challenged the commission's refusal to hear complaints in connection with license renewals. The FCC was propelled into regulating employment as links were made between unrepresentative programs and the mostly white, male profile of the radio and television industries, and it was pressured to investigate the needs of groups such as children and handicapped persons. During this time, growing numbers of groups and individuals participated in FCC proceedings, even proposing new regulations that were made part of the agency's agenda.

Before Fowler became chairman, some members of Congress and industry groups tried to stop this activity and throw communications regulation back to the marketplace. The commission under Fowler, which included a total of four Reagan appointees, succeeded in accelerating the deregulatory process through changes in procedures as well as in the much-maligned regulations.

Public groups found themselves asked to do the equivalent of breaking down walls in order to obtain information about the commission's actions. Summaries of meetings, press releases, notices of proceedings, and final orders that previously had been sent to dozens of groups free of charge were collapsed into a one- or two-page bulletin called the Daily Digest, which was of little use without additional documentation. Materials about proceedings had to be purchased from a privately run copy center. The delay caused by having to write in and wait for the order to be processed, more than the fee involved, made it more difficult to comment on proposed rules in a timely manner, particularly since the comment periods on many important issues were shorter than in the past.

In general, public inquiries met with a rude and opaque response. Attempts to obtain straightforward factual information necessitated repeated telephone calls and carefully framed questions. Either on account of poor training or an unwillingness to provide information, often no one was available who could be of assistance or even suggest another place to call. On at least one occasion, in the course of a major proceeding on the deregulation of commercial television, a commission employee admitted that relevant information that had recently been published by the commission in its rules volumes was not correct. Hence, it was entirely conceivable that commission personnel were giving out the wrong answers.

Few people were prepared to proceed under such difficulties and over long-distance telephone lines. In the midst of an historic era of change in the communications field, the chief policy-making body was doing everything possible to silence discussion.

One example of the commission's disinterest in collecting information is particularly impressive. In 1981, radio and television stations were told they were no longer obliged to fill out application forms of ten to twenty pages for renewal of their licenses. Those forms had provided the commission as well as the public with information about station service and needs of the community. In the new rule, stations only had to fill out postcards that indicated whether or not they were in compliance with FCC regulations.

This change was heralded by the Office of Management and Budget in its end-of-year review of government paperwork reductions. The same year, the OMB also celebrated the elimination of an FCC requirement that radio stations submit program logs that provided examples of their program schedules and were the most effective means for community members to gather information necessary to file comments. The District of Columbia Court of Appeals reversed this commission action, stating that the FCC was not allowed to remove critical information from public purview, much less to withdraw itself so completely from its own obligations to oversee stations.

Converting requirements for hearings to requirements for paperwork is a neat way of lessening public participation. By the same token, eliminating form-filing and record-keeping requirements can facilitate dramatic reductions in an agency's work load without the bother of justifying major changes in regulations that have, in effect, been suspended. The operations of the FCC during the Reagan administration were replete with examples whereby both these tactics were used to maximum benefit. It is little wonder, then, that the FCC was regarded as a model agency in the eyes of high-level officials, the Heritage Foundation, and other zealous proponents of deregulation.

Chapter 5

OVERSIGHT UNDERMINED
Congress Refused Vital Information

In the Reagan era, Congress was both the victim of the administration's preference for secrecy and the perpetrator of new obstacles to informed public debate. Most of the information restrictions initiated in the early 1980's were introduced by the executive branch. Numerous congressional committees met with resistance and antagonism in their attempts to communicate with the Justice Department and other agencies, while, at the same time, regulatory programs legislated by Congress were endangered by the closed operations of the executive branch. Congress, too, however, enacted laws that limited access to public information.

The overall opinions of Congress regarding important issues of classification and government responsibility for the provision of information are difficult to assess, as there are 535 elected members, holding a wide range of perspectives. Serious differences of opinion exist among them over the public versus the private nature of information, the desirability of releasing technical or product information to the public, and any number of other issues relevant to federal information policy. Even with regard to congressional action, no clear line of policy is evident. Often the more significant actions of Congress in the area of information policy have been responses to actual or perceived public demands. Congress also has widened public access at times when it was encountering resistance from other departments in its own attempts to gather information. Following revelations of domestic surveillance by the CIA and White House transgressions in the Nixon era, for example, Congress put pressure on the White House to curtail the powers of the intelligence agencies and strengthened the Freedom of Information Act as a tool for public investigation.

The 1980 Paperwork Reduction Act made cutting down on paperwork more important than disclosing information, perhaps inadvertently, as it contained no criteria for agencies to apply in deciding what documents to retain. As Reagan's term began, paperwork reduction was available as a legitimate basis for discarding agency record-keeping rules that not only provided the public with valuable information but were essential to effective enforcement of regulations. Moreover, as Congress became preoccupied with military spending and the conservative shift in the political climate, it looked entirely possible that legislators would go along with sweeping limitations on civil liberties and access to information in the same way they had embraced Reagan's tax and spending cuts for fiscal year 1982.

In 1981, more than thirty bills were introduced to amend the FOIA. They seemed part of a broader attempt to inhibit political activity by groups and individuals. During the same year that the CIA sought and obtained an executive order authorizing it to spy on Americans who were thought to be involved in subversive organizations, to open mail without a warrant, and to infiltrate political organizations inside the United States,[1] the Senate Judiciary Committee established a new Subcommittee on Security and Terrorism, which was chaired by Sen. Jeremiah Denton of Alabama. Subcommittee members expressed serious interest in monitoring political groups in the country for signs of Soviet infiltration and international terrorism. In the House, the late Larry McDonald of Georgia sponsored a resolution to establish a Committee on National Security with the sole function of investigating allegedly subversive domestic groups. Legislation was introduced and passed the following year that made it a crime to disclose the identity of intelligence agents even if the information was obtained from an unclassified source.

FREEDOM OF INFORMATION ACT LEGISLATION

The Freedom of Information Act was passed in 1966 and strengthened in 1974 to change a system that permitted access to government records only for people deemed "directly and properly concerned" and "for good cause found." The FOIA principle is that the public has a right to know, apart from subjective decisions by government officials, and unless refusals to provide requested documents are justified by law. Some of the initial proposals to amend the FOIA that were introduced in 1981 would have contradicted this constitutionally based rule and significantly weakened the act.

Sen. Orrin Hatch of Utah took the lead, proposing amendments that would have allowed law enforcement agencies to withhold information about investigations of organized crime, exempted most business records, and given the U.S. attorney general new power to exempt all information relating to terrorism and foreign counterintelligence. In addition, Hatch's original bill authorized agencies to charge steep fees for FOIA searches and copying and even created an exemption for papers relating to people who had been deceased less than twenty-five years. Hatch's bill closely resembled White House proposals that were clearly designed to destroy the FOIA's effectiveness.

These proposals and others to exempt all records of CIA operations encountered strong opposition from the press, the academic community, and an alliance of public groups, including the Organization of American Historians, the Fund for Open Information and Accountability, Inc., and Common Cause. The press lobby included representatives of the American Newspaper Publishers' Association, the National Association of Broadcasters, the Reporters' Committee for Freedom of the Press, and the Society of Professional Journalists, Sigma Delta Chi.

Some critics of the FOIA maintained that the act was not often used by the press. This argument was soundly refuted in testimony that provided many examples of investigative stories that could not have been written without documents obtained under the act. CBS news correspondent Bob Schieffer, testifying on behalf of the Society of Professional Journalists, pointed out that the act was frequently used by reporters who did not declare their press affiliations. Moreover, he said, "Statistics do not reflect the enormous amount of information received from the mere presence of having this act on the books. Any journalist can give illustrations from personal experience about how agencies voluntarily disgorge information at the mere mention of a possible Freedom of Information Act request."[2]

Opposition to FOIA restrictions quickly emerged in Congress. Sen. Patrick Leahy of Vermont led the effort to defend the act and countered the initial Hatch proposals, while Rep. Glenn English of Oklahoma insisted on hearings on the proposed legislation. By the end of 1982, a compromise had been reached that deleted or limited many of the original exemption proposals. By that time, many members had lost interest in significant amendment of the FOIA.

Through less direct legislative action, however, exemptions were added to the act, largely without public knowledge. This modification was accomplished through an often overlooked provision of the FOIA that allows agencies to turn down FOIA requests for material that is specifically exempted by other laws covering agency programs. Exemptions adopted under this provision—commonly referred to by its number, b(3)—do not go through the usual FOIA committee process. Rather, they originate in committees dealing with authorization bills or other matters unrelated to information policy. Notices in the *Congressional Record* do not always indicate that a new secrecy law is being reviewed. The b(3) amendments receive no public hearings and tend to pass easily with the main legislation. Not even final passage of an exemption is publicized. This information can escape public attention for months or even years, since no comprehensive list of b(3) exemptions exists. These exemptions usually come to light once an agency relies upon one to deny a FOIA request.

Between 1980 and 1984, Congress adopted at least six significant b(3) exemptions. The first, exempting Federal Trade Commission (FTC) investigations, became a model for other agencies seeking to remove agency proceedings from public scrutiny. After that, Congress adopted laws that exempted information submitted by manufacturers of hazardous products to the Consumer Product Safety Commission (CPSC); unclassified information submitted to the Department of Energy about the production and transportation of nuclear materials; the records of professional review standards organizations that review the medical practices of institutions relying on medicaid funding dispersed by the Department of Health and Human Services; and information about nuclear research gathered by the Nuclear Regulatory Commission.

Such exemptions could dramatically affect agency responses to FOIA requests. According to Tonda Rush, a lawyer at the American Newspaper Publishers' Association, after the CPSC hazardous-product information exemption was passed, the agency's FOIA office output diminished.[3] In addition, the exemptions strained relations between the agencies and major research institutions. This happened when the Department of Energy released proposed regulations to apply the FOIA restriction on the dissemination of unclassified nuclear information to material held by nongovernmental libraries.[4] Stanford University was among dozens of academic and scientific institutions to protest this action on the grounds that it would impair their ability to conduct important basic research under government grants. In its written comment on this issue, Stanford said, "We do not have the ability—nor, indeed, would we be willing—to search our documents or censor our classes for material that might, under the very vague proposed standards, constitute Unclassified Controlled Nuclear Information, with the futile and repugnant object of making known and unclassified information secret."

Hugh DeWitt, a scientist on the staff of a nuclear weapons design laboratory in Livermore, California, accused the Department of Energy of misleading the public by pretending that information covered by the proposed regulations would be unclassified while, in fact, a new level of classification was being created. DeWitt criticized the rule for giving Department of Energy officials free rein to suppress information about the adverse health effects on humans resulting from past and present nuclear testing.

The proposal also came under fire from unions, environmental groups, library organizations, and numerous congressional representatives. Nolan Hancock of the Oil, Chemical, and Atomic Workers' Union testified at a Department of Energy hearing that the agency's plan would unjustifiably deny nuclear industry workers access to information on potential health hazards. Sandra Petersen of the American Library Association said the plan would create a nightmare for libraries, forcing them to ask the Department of Energy for permission every time an individual wanted access to "any one of thousands of documents."[5] And, objecting to the unwanted consequences of a b(3) exemption of their own making, sixteen members of the House wrote the secretary of the Department of Energy that its proposal exceeded its statutory authority to classify and would deprive lawmakers and the public of vital information.[6]

"NAMING NAMES"—THE IDENTITIES INTELLIGENCE PROTECTION ACT OF 1982

On issues related to foreign policy and national security, Congress has traditionally gone along with the policies set by the White House. In late 1983, legislation established the Institute for Democracy, which was part of Reagan's Project Democracy (see chapter 2). Since the institute was set up as a private organization, it was not covered by the FOIA.

A similar tolerance for secrecy in such matters was evident in a 1982 bill that prescribed penalties for present and former officials with access to intelligence information who disclosed the identities of intelligence agents. It also made it illegal for private persons to engage in activities intended to expose covert agents. Names that had already been published were not exempted, nor was information that revealed illegal conduct of intelligence officials.[7] This legislation had been debated for several years, as the CIA and its allies in Congress pressed for a way to stop activists such as Philip Agee and the editors of *Covert Action Information Bulletin* from reporting on intelligence operations. CIA Director William Casey argued that a few people with the avowed purpose of destroying the effectiveness of government intelligence gathering were endangering the work of U.S. foreign intelligence.

Press groups and civil libertarians reacted to the CIA's position by maintaining that it was unconstitutional for names derived from public documents to be the basis of criminal penalties. They saw the CIA's efforts as an attempt to prevent legitimate monitoring of government misconduct by citizens. Jack Landau, executive director of the Reporters' Committee for Freedom of the Press, testified that "to convict reporters, to jail editors, or to fine publishers for naming a government intelligence employee who is violating the law or the public policy statements of the President is too high a price to pay in the name of national security."[8]

The legislation that was finally passed was accompanied by a report that indicated that regular press reporting would not be prosecutable; to be blameworthy, persons had to be in the business of naming names. Nonetheless, the bill's actual impact depended on who relied on it to punish what kinds of behavior. Since such legislation is unlikely to affect Soviet intelligence one way or another, the central issue is whether there was adequate justification for sweeping new secrecy legislation that could severely inhibit important reporting of government activities.

EXECUTIVE BRANCH REFUSAL TO SHARE INFORMATION

According to numerous congressional aides and public groups involved in legislative activity, conflict between the executive branch and Congress during the Reagan administration went beyond the usual level of tension between two branches of government. Committee requests for information from different agencies frequently met with long delays, red tape, and incomplete responses. When the White House was drafting new classification guidelines, invitations from Congress to discuss them with committees were ignored until after the president's order had been signed. Regular briefings that intelligence officials had traditionally given committee members involved in determining appropriation levels for national defense ended shortly after Reagan took office. Furthermore, there is a virtually endless list of examples of agency personnel refusing to cooperate with congressional oversight and investigations. In 1983, when a House committee repeatedly sought information from several agencies about actions being taken to deal with the outbreak of the Acquired Immune Deficiency Syndrome (AIDS), its requests were turned down. Even when a staff investigator made a trip to the office of the Center for Disease Control in Atlanta, she was told that no information could be released unless specifically requested in writing.

DEPARTMENT OF THE INTERIOR

Some of these information requests led to protracted battles over committee access to agency records. Beginning in July 1981, the House Committee on Energy and Commerce was involved in a year-long ordeal to convince the secretary of the interior to share documents during an investigation of charges that Canadian companies were using unfair advantages contained in Canadian law to acquire American energy companies. Secretary James Watt instructed his staff not to communicate with committee members. This dispute led to claims of executive privilege, which were denounced by the general counsel of the House as grossly overstated and legally unsubstantiated. In time, Watt was declared in contempt of Congress by votes in the investigating subcommittee and then in the full committee. At one point, White House counsel offered to share the desired documents only with the committee chairman and the senior Republican committee member. This offer was refused on the grounds that all members were entitled to view the material. Finally, a vote of contempt by the entire House was narrowly averted when the White House sent over the documents for a four-hour period in which agreed upon conditions limited the manner in which information could be copied from the documents submitted.

In a committee report issued at the end of this episode, an attempt was made to account for the administration's behavior.[9] "There seems to be a concerted effort by this Administration to reduce and control access to governmental information in the hands of the Executive," the report stated. "Over the past several months, other Congressional Committees have encountered increasing difficulties in obtaining information requested for governmental agencies. A Justice Department attorney told Committee staff that the Administration sought to develop a 'consistent policy' for dealing with Committee requests. Some agency administrators have purported to establish ground rules regarding the conduct of Committee inquiries into agency activities, including prohibitions on staff interviews. Such a policy may be welcome for agency administrators who seek to avoid being held accountable for their actions, but it is damaging to an honest, efficient, and democratic government."[10]

At a later date, the Interior Department again resisted committee requests for information, this time with regard to plans for the sale of public lands. Agency staff stonewalled, insisting they lacked information as to what lands had been put on sale or sold. Brooks Yaeger of the Sierra Club said that this claim of ignorance was merely pretense. "I think they've purposely refused to centralize the information and kept it at district offices so that groups like ourselves can be refused access," he said.[11] James Norton of the Wilderness Society suggested that the main motivation for these inter-agency duels was the delight in battle. According to him, at least one person was employed full-time at the Department of the Interior to find loopholes in the underlying legislation. Norton said, "At one point this person tried to open four million acres of national wildlife refuges to oil and gas leasing by reinterpreting a sentence that was missing a comma!" But in this instance, Congress caught on quickly.

"Moreover," said Norton, "once a loophole was discovered, Watt would try to drive a truck through it."[12]

On yet another occasion, Congress got wind of a plan to sell 2.7 million acres of land and attempted to obtain from the Interior Department, copies of preliminary analyses and targeted areas. This request was turned down by the agency, which claimed the documents did not exist. The agency's deceit was immediately apparent, however, because an agency employee had leaked the requested documents to the chairman of the Public Lands and National Parks Subcommittee, Rep. John Seiberling of Ohio.

By the time he resigned in 1983, Watt had compiled a record of flagrant disregard of congressional oversight and unceasing contempt for his agency's statutory mandate.

ENVIRONMENTAL PROTECTION AGENCY

After the administration's first year, heads of other agencies generated similar controversies. In 1982, the Environmental Protection Agency administrator, Anne Gorsuch Burford, became the first Cabinet-level official in history to be cited for contempt of Congress. This citation was based on Burford's refusal to comply with a subpoena covering documents the EPA had on 160 hazardous-waste sites given priority for cleanup under emergency legislation passed in 1980. By the end of an acrimonious ten-month battle involving the EPA, the Justice Department, the White House, and six congressional committees, strong evidence had been gathered indicating that the agency had colluded with companies dumping hazardous wastes to avoid meeting statutory deadlines for dump clearance. Several EPA employees had connections with regulated companies that created conflict of interest with their official obligations.

Normally the Justice Department would have been responsible for helping the agency and the committee to work out their differences. In this instance, it consistently made recommendations guaranteed to escalate a dispute over agency records into a full-scale constitutional confrontation. The arguments it provided for the defense of executive privilege here were similar to those it had put forward earlier for the Department of the Interior: the Constitution implied a privilege of the executive to ensure the confidentiality of presidential law enforcement and policy deliberation.

This line of reasoning was a grand overstatement of the grounds for executive privilege that had been outlined in the 1974 Supreme Court decision ordering Richard Nixon to turn White House tapes over to the Watergate prosecutors. Chief Justice Warren E. Burger, writing for the court, said, "Nowhere in the Constitution . . . is there any explicit reference to a privilege of confidentiality, yet to the extent this interest relates to the effective discharge of a President's powers, it is constitutionally based."[13] Nonetheless, Nixon lost his case because the court ruled that the importance of the ongoing Watergate prosecution outweighed his "generalized interest in confidentiality" of his communications.

Unlike the Nixon claim, the EPA's assertion of executive privilege did not involve personal, presidential communication but, instead, an agency within the executive branch trying to keep certain documents from the legislature. Moreover, upon questioning, EPA General Counsel Robert Perry admitted that the president had not seen the contested material. Not surprisingly, the counsel for the House responded with a direct statement that the law of executive privilege did not allow claims of privilege unless the president had actually seen the documents he was so eager to protect.

After Burford was voted in contempt of Congress in December 1982, the Justice Department unsuccessfully filed suit against Congress, still pursuing the administration's argument of executive privilege, to forestall further action by the committee to obtain documents that had still not been sent to them. This quest for congressional submission on the part of the attorney general, the nation's highest law-enforcement officer, did not escape committee attention. During the hearings on the hazardous-waste program following Burford's resignation, a memorandum from the Justice Department to the White House was produced in which a department official recommended that Reagan order the head of the EPA to assert the claim of executive privilege on behalf of the president.[14] Burford testified that, on her own, she would have submitted the requested documents and had argued against the strategies she was compelled to adopt.

This incident may have been one of the darkest chapters in the history of relations between these two branches of government. Invalid and unnecessary legal claims were presented for the sole purpose of preventing Congress from carrying out its constitutionally mandated obligation to see that appropriated funds had been used for right and lawful purposes.

FEDERAL COMMUNICATIONS AND
FEDERAL TRADE COMMISSIONS

In other agencies, such as the Federal Communications Commission and the Federal Trade Commission, officials carrying out policies of deregulation resisted congressional scrutiny of their actions. These officials frequently claimed that information requested by Congress did not exist—which, if it was true, was an admission of mismanagement—or refused to answer direct questions posed by the legislators.

When the House was attempting to draft new communications legislation for broadcasting, requests for data on station compliance with existing FCC regulation were turned down with the answer "not available." Meanwhile, in testimony before the Communications Subcommittee, Chairman Mark Fowler did a two-step around direct questions regarding the FCC's plan to deregulate television, as the following excerpt indicates:

MR. WIRTH. Let me jump, if I might, to a recent court of appeals decision. The court of appeals, in its recent radio deregulation decision, stated, "It should thus be Congress, and not the unrepresentative bureaucracy and judiciary, that takes the lead in grossly amending that system," referring to the system of broadcast regulation, "thereby providing the public with a greater voice in this important process."

Do you agree with the court in that statement?

MR. FOWLER. Yes, sir.

MR. WIRTH. Would you agree, then, that the FCC should withhold on TV deregulation, particularly given the fact that we are now deeply embroiled in the Congress in this process?

MR. FOWLER. Withhold—

MR. WIRTH. FCC action on television deregulation?

MR. FOWLER. I wouldn't say that we will withhold that action, sir, but certainly we will be very sensitive to your concerns. I don't see anything wrong, however, in moving forward to ask those questions. . . .

MR. WIRTH. Let me point out that you have indicated that the Commission intends to deregulate television along the lines of radio deregulation.

This would involve the FCC abolishing its processing guidelines. It seems to me that, given your agreement with what the court said, and given the process that we are undergoing, that it would be inappropriate for the FCC to do that while the Congress is considering this quantification legislation.

MR. FOWLER. I don't think I said that we were going to effect TV deregulation along the lines of radio and television. I think I said we were going to in the very near term institute a proceeding to consider whether we ought to move along the lines of what we did in radio deregulation.

I don't think there has been any decision by the Commission about the ultimate conclusion of such a proceeding.

MR. WIRTH. As one chairman to another, you heard me, right?[15]

A dispute also evolved between the head of the Federal Trade Commission, James Miller, and the head of the House Energy and Commerce Committee, Rep. John Dingell of Michigan, which demonstrated the arrogance typical of a number of Reagan-appointed agency executives.

In 1981 Miller asked Congress to change the statutory standards for FTC action against deceptive industry practices in a way that would have made it harder for consumers to file a prosecutable complaint. When he was flatly turned down in both the House and the Senate, he and his fellow commissioners ignored the will of Congress and made the changes through revisions of agency enforcement guidelines. When Dingell became aware of what was happening, he put Miller on notice by requesting from him an historical analysis of consumer-protection law dating back fifty years. In response, Miller ignored the substance of the committee chairman's request and the underlying message and merely submitted a description of current FTC plans and policies. Shortly thereafter, he boldly challenged one of the most powerful members of Congress by holding a press conference in which he ridiculed Dingell's oversight authority and announced that he had no intention of cooperating with the committee.

A key issue here was Miller's attempt to change the law of consumer protection through deliberately misinterpreting the law. One congressional source who was close to this situation said, "Congress can't change what Miller is doing, but through engagement of vigorous oversight it can ensure that this criteria [sic] are not elevated to legal evidentiary status. This is a classic case of an administrative agency pitted against Congress."

CONGRESSIONAL REMEDIES

There is no way short of impeachment for Congress to exact full accountability from an uncooperative agency executive. Investigations and oversight, however, are often used effectively to apply pressure. In the spring of 1983, Congress reacted swiftly to the presidential directive that imposed a sweeping system of prior review on more than 100,000 present and former government employees. That same year, both the House and Senate issued a moratorium on the directive's implementation. (After that, the administration announced its own temporary suspension of the directive.) In general, after the honeymoon of the Reagan administration was over, many Democratic members of Congress began to look more critically at the plans of the administration. Committees sent regular, carefully framed requests for information to the agencies in their charge and held regular hearings. It is perhaps no exaggeration to say that records and letters and other documentary materials were at the center of a mounting struggle between the objectives of the executive branch and Congress.

Congress also applied the power of the purse. To ensure that funds appropriated to the Office of Management and Budget were used to upgrade federal statistics, it included a provision requiring that the position of chief statistician, which had been left vacant by the OMB for more than a year, be filled. The administration's first budget proposals had moved without much fuss. After that, Congress began to make independent judgments about cutbacks in different areas, including matters of research and the of agency information. In 1982, for example, it substantially more for the Consumer Product mission than the administration had requested tional funds went toward broadening the agenc   ....o- sure of information and retaining a board that advised companies on providing first-aid instructions on product labels. Other agency programs were also expanded. Money for the EPA's research and investigation efforts, which had been cut back in 1981 and 1982, was restored.

During Reagan's term, Congress was often besieged by more than the usual number of both the petty and significant conflicts that have traditionally characterized relations between the legislative and executive branches. This situation was due to the administration's arrogant view that the executive branch was *the* government and should share information about its activities only when it was convenient. Consequently, many times Congress issued or came close to issuing subpoenas in attempts to gather materials that certainly could not pass the test of executive privilege but had been withheld as part of an agency's persistent challenge to congressional authority. Much of the combat that ensued may have been unavoidable. However, on important matters such as public access to unclassified documents and the obligation of agencies to provide information, Congress could have done more to halt executive secrecy by adopting policies and criteria for the disclosure of information. Furthermore, it might have looked into the growing tension between information disclosure and paperwork reduction.

Chapter 6

DRYING UP THE SOURCE
Assault on the Media

I KNOW THE PRESS ONLY TOO WELL. AL-
MOST ALL EDITORS HIDE AWAY IN SPIDER-
DENS, MEN WITHOUT THOUGHT OF FAMILY
OR PUBLIC INTEREST OR THE HUMBLE DE-
LIGHTS OF JAUNTS OUT-OF-DOORS, PLOT-
TING HOW THEY CAN PUT OVER THEIR LIES,
AND ADVANCE THEIR OWN POSITIONS AND
FILL THEIR GREEDY POCKETBOOKS BY
CALUMNIATING STATESMEN WHO HAVE
GIVEN THEIR ALL FOR THE COMMON GOOD
AND WHO ARE VULNERABLE BECAUSE THEY
STAND OUT IN THE FIERCE LIGHT THAT
BEATS AROUND THE THRONE.

—Berzelius Windrip in
It Can't Happen Here
by Sinclair Lewis, 1938

Over the last decade, the American media rose high in
public esteem following the Watergate revelations and,
shortly thereafter, were taken to the woodshed where they
were castigated for a multitude of alleged transgressions,
including elitism and lack of patriotism. Such fluctuations,
though more extreme than would ordinarily be expected in
a ten-year period, were nonetheless part of the everyday

90

life of the media. Thriving to some extent on license and eccentricity, and covering issues of great importance in a land of diverse political interests, the media have always been the subject of ambivalent public attitudes.

During the same period that public complaints increased, however, the Reagan administration took unprecedented steps to restrict the press, through executive orders, legislative proposals, and tight controls on contacts between reporters and government personnel. Government campaigns to "reform" the media are much more suspect than those emanating from the public. Traditionally, the public obtains its primary information about the government from two sources: the media and the government. By restricting the access of the press to the government the administration diminished the accountability of political leaders, with wide-ranging implications.

A vivid example of how democracy can be converted into autocracy through the suppression of the media was presented by Sinclair Lewis in his novel of the 1930's *It Can't Happen Here.* The novel's central character, Berzelius Windrip, skillfully employed populist rhetoric in praise of the common man to become president of the United States. Once elected, he quickly cracked down on anyone who was not totally subservient to his will. One of Windrip's first acts as president was to jail a popular radio announcer. He then proceeded to replace all journalists and editors with his own puppet press.

President Reagan, while hardly the despotic ruler of Lewis' novel, also sought to weaken permanently the power of the press. In his attempts to institutionalize long-term restrictions, he can be distinguished from the many presidents before him who railed against the media but did not seek to enact restrictions into law. Richard Nixon, for example, for whom journalists were a persistent headache, eventually had intelligence agents wiretapping reporters' telephone lines, opening their mail, and raiding press offices. Such measures were believed to have ended when Nixon left office. The Reagan administration also authorized the FBI and CIA to search newsrooms and instituted a stream of ad hoc restrictions. It was primarily interested, however, in designing laws and regulations that would outlast the administration and reposition the media as a subordinated source of information about the actions of government.

RESTRICTED CONVERSATION WITH OFFICIALS

From the beginning of the Reagan administration, restrictions were imposed on contacts between government officials and the media.[1] Early on, the CIA ended its practice of providing background briefings to reporters on unclassified intelligence information. Shortly thereafter, a presidential directive ordered all employees of the executive branch to obtain clearance before speaking with reporters about foreign policy or national-security issues. This action evoked strong opposition and was soon withdrawn, to be replaced by more narrowly drawn restrictions. Rules were imposed requiring National Security Council staff to sign nondisclosure forms and limiting the number of White House officials who were permitted to meet with journalists.

Informal conversations were increasingly the subject of regulation. At one point, Defense Secretary Casper Weinberger called for prior screening procedures for breakfast meetings between reporters and Pentagon officials. Following reports that Reagan advisers had obtained briefing materials from the Carter camp during the 1980 presidential campaign season, the head of the FBI Washington, D.C., office was abruptly transferred to Portland, Oregon, when it was discovered that he had spoken to reporters about the bureau's plans to investigate the matter.

At the heart of the administration's policies here was an inordinate impatience with the decentralized relationships that existed between members of the Fourth Estate and officials scattered throughout the federal government. Included were day-to-day conversations that took place off the record, informal networks of information sharing, and the exchange of favors built upon years of dealing between career civil servants and the press. Clearly, to end or even significantly to weaken these customs and relationships required both intricate plans and artful explanation.

The impact of the government's secrecy measures was softened for public consumption by Reagan's Hollywood-nurtured charm. Reagan had a rare ability to direct public attention away from himself on awkward issues and toward himself for strictly personal conversation. He would often entertain audiences with storylike references to "When I was young . . ." or "I recently received a letter from a young man who . . ." It was not long before he began being described as the Great Communicator, appearing regularly on prime-time television. Such family-hour presentations served to hide the fact that he held many fewer press conferences than did most other presidents and did poorly in question-and-answer situations.

On those occasions when he agreed to take questions, Reagan made numerous factual mistakes.[2] It became known that his aides tried hard to prevent him from giving spontaneous answers to reporters' questions. On numerous occasions, they held sessions after press conferences to minimize Reagan's errors by explaining what he had meant to say.

A consistent attribute of administration officials was a studied indifference to the value of factual information. Facts were presented merely as addenda to major policy decisions. Often it seemed they were eliminated in order to direct people to ideological goals of greater importance or, better yet, to make government plans easier to digest. This is always true to some extent, but Reagan's policies were more heavily laden with ideology than those of other administrations. Eliminating factual materials made it that much more difficult for groups and individuals to respond effectively to policy changes that were taking place. Depending on how far such fact omission was carried, the media and political discussion generally could become a charade. Charles Rowe alluded to this frightening possibility when he testified on the administration's classification order on behalf of the American Newspaper Publishers' Association and the Society of Newspaper Editors. Rowe stated, "If this unwise 'philosophy of closure' were to triumph in Washington, it soon would trickle down to state governments, local courts and school boards and our society would change."[3]

Unfortunately, the administration forged ahead to institute the very sort of change that Rowe and many others dreaded. Many of its efforts to control communication culminated in the presidential directive of March 1983 that established governmentwide lie detector examinations and made more than 120,000 current and former officials subject to prior review of their speeches and writings. An interagency team headed by Richard Willard in the Department of Justice spent over a year examining possibilities for strengthening central authority over the release of information. The plan they finally decided on, National Security Directive 84, was essentially a law-enforcement system within the federal government. Agencies were instructed to develop rules for monitoring their contacts with the press, and both civilian and criminal penalties were enacted for violators.

In an interview with the *Washington Post,* Willard admitted that the directive was unlikely to curtail significantly the number of instances in which information vital to the national security was disclosed. The main purpose of the directive, he said, was to foster a better attitude among government employees by means of intimidation. "Leaks are consensual crimes," Willard told the *Post.* Potential criminals would be deterred if appropriate punishments were established.

Under such conditions, the line separating regulated communication and authoritarian rule is quite faint. Willard's apparent lack of concern for this fundamental issue was a clear reflection of the Reagan administration's disdain for First Amendment freedoms of speech and press.

THE FREEDOM OF INFORMATION ACT

For journalists, the FOIA has been an indispensable means of obtaining unclassified documents. For the Reagan administration, it was an enemy within its own ranks. One of the first acts of then Attorney General William French Smith was to reverse Carter-era guidelines, which instructed agencies to release information unless a clear threat to national security could be identified. The White House also attempted to undermine the FOIA by submitting proposals to Congress that records on intelligence operations, business, organized crime investigations, and other subjects be exempted from the act. After a while, the likelihood of Congress passing such legislation looked slim, and efforts were intensified to weaken the FOIA through restrictions by the executive branch.

The president's order on classification that was issued in 1982 significantly limited the volume of information available under the FOIA by requiring that agency doubts over classification be resolved in favor of the highest possible level of classification.[4] Under Carter, agencies had been given discretionary authority in this area. They would often release documents that might be classified if they found that such release would only minimally damage national security. Reagan's order ruled out this flexibility.

In addition, the order created two broad, new subject categories[5] and introduced a presumption in favor of classifying certain intelligence information. The latter restriction came at the same time that the CIA was given new authorization to infiltrate domestic groups suspected of terrorist connections.[6] Domestic intelligence is an area where Congress has always relied heavily on the media for its own information.

Furthermore, the cost of obtaining FOIA documents was raised to a point where it was often tantamount to a denial of access. The act itself states that costs for searching and copying material should be reduced or waived if that would serve the public interest. Reporters are among those specifically mentioned as likely to qualify for reduced fees. But, according to the fee guidelines issued by the Reagan Justice Department, no waivers could be granted unless requests met a stringent five-part test. Agency officials were to judge (1) whether the subject matter was of public interest; (2) how valuable disparate materials were to the request; (3) the identity and qualifications of the individual requesting materials; and (4) that individual's personal interest. Moreover, (5) records that could be obtained elsewhere, even if in far away places, were to be withheld.[7] Some of these criteria had been rejected by the courts, while nearly all were in conflict with the liberal disclosure policy adopted by Congress.

Still another impediment to the FOIA was erected when several agencies, including the Environmental Protection Agency and the Justice Department, began requiring that people submitting requests pay in advance for the cost of searching and copying documents. Costs were estimated at market rates, and some journalists were asked to advance as much as a thousand dollars before they or the agency had a clear sense of how many documents could be located.

Some agencies gained a reputation for summarily rejecting all FOIA requests until the appeals level. Others per-

fected the art of delaying disclosure long past the date for
scheduled publication of an article or completion of an
academic report. Edward Cony, an executive of Dow
Jones, wrote an article questioning what value remained in
FOIA procedures under these circumstances.[8] Cony described an episode in which *Wall Street Journal* reporters
requested documents in connection with an agreement between the United States and Egypt for the transfer of air-
planes and military equipment. The Pentagon initially
identified more than twenty thousand relevant documents
but refused to release any of them. The *Journal* story appeared without benefit of government records. Months
later, as the company pursued its request, it learned that the
material had been marked for "retroactive classification."
Finally, twenty-five documents were released. One of them
was the *Journal* article that prompted the initial request and
was now labeled declassified government information.

One particularly clever attempt by the administration to
dilute the strength of the FOIA was through claiming that
certain material was exempted by the Privacy Act of 1974.
These two laws overlap to some limited extent and were
generally understood not to be in conflict.[9] The Privacy Act
exempted certain law-enforcement records, and in 1981,
the attorney general sought to use this exemption to prevent the disclosure of information concerning the CIA and
FBI that had been requested under the FOIA.

Apart from this being a new strategy, what is interesting
here is the way in which the Privacy Act was being used for
purposes in direct conflict with its objectives. Congress had
passed the act after discovering that intelligence agencies
had illegally wiretapped and seized records from public
groups, including the press, during the Nixon years. One of
the act's explicit objectives was to provide protection
against illegal attempts by the government to seize private
information. Then, in 1983, the Justice Department issued
regulations re-authorizing intelligence agencies to search

pressrooms.[10] Ostensibly, the Privacy Act should have provided protection against abuse of this authority; however, because of the Justice Department's own use of the Privacy Act to exempt intelligence information, discovery that agencies had exceeded their lawful authority was less likely.

NEWS COVERAGE OF GRENADA

The U.S. invasion of Grenada in October 1983 was a historic moment in the relationship between the government and the media, as well as between the media and the American public. Because of its short duration and the relatively few lives lost in battle, the episode bore little resemblance to a major military event. It was a major national event, however, for two reasons. It was the first time that U.S. troops had been sent abroad for a combat attack since the Vietnam War, and it was the first invasion in U.S. history in which the media were absent during the initial fighting.

At the outset, military reports relayed to Washington and adapted for the media were the only accounts of the invasion available to the public. Three days later, and once most of the fighting had ended, small pools of reporters were admitted under highly unusual conditions. Each day, from the dozens of journalists stationed in Barbados, a small group would be selected to be taken on a guided tour of Grenada, following an itinerary that had been approved in advance by military officials. During this time, Washington was not providing important information, including the number of American and Cuban lives lost in the invasion. For six days, the bombing of a civilian hospital went unreported.

Later on, some of the information that had been provided

was found to be inaccurate. Weapon caches were found to contain less modern and less lethal military hardware than had previously been attested. Claims that the lives of American students on the island had been in grave danger were disproven by independent confirmation that they had been promised by Grenada safe transport home.[11] United States government estimates of the number of Cuban troops on the island were challenged and revised more than once.

As a result, a tidal wave of criticism by the press and television and radio network executives came roaring down from all over the country. The media had been outraged at their exclusion and maintained that the public had a constitutional right to news gathered by a nongovernmental source. In the past, the press had been allowed to accompany troops on military actions. When necessary, reporters had agreed to delay sending dispatches until maneuvers had been completed. Media executives insisted that the government had provided no convincing reason why similar arrangements could not have been arranged in Grenada.

Henry Grunwald, editor-in-chief of Time, Inc., wrote a stinging editorial entitled "Trying to Censor Reality."[12] Grunwald summarized the essence of media objections in his statement, "Taken together, the administration's measures suggest a certain mindset: the notion that events can be shaped by their presentation, that truth should be a controlled substance." Dozens of other editors, television commentators, and First Amendment lawyers likewise raised strong objections to the administration's actions regarding the press.[13]

The public, however, did not seem to mind their lack of information and gave media protest little support. Indeed, it seemed that the more eloquent media objections to restricting their access to information became, the louder the public shot insults at the media, calling them elitist, unpatriotic, irresponsible, and a string of other unpleasantries. Why did the public react so violently against their investigative arm? And why did they seem to lose interest so quickly in the circumstances of the Grenadian invasion and in the occupation, which lasted many months longer than the government had proposed?

From the standpoint of the media, the entire situation felt like an assault from ahead and from behind. They were first required to scale the fortress wall—fully justifying their every movement by reference to the public's right to know. Then, when the public seemed to turn on *them,* they had to defend themselves against this unexpected attack from the rear.

It is possible that the public reaction was a cumulative one, the aggregate of grievances that had festered for a long time. The number of libel suits had increased greatly since the end of the 1960's; the public had grown more impatient with the insensitivity of reporters who shoved microphones at people downed in airplane tragedies or in other situations of human suffering. Yet this, alone, would not explain why, while people were lambasting reporters, they were not also pestering the government for better information about Grenada.

Another explanation to be considered is that the press may gradually have become a whipping post because of the president's skillful way of deflecting public discontent away from himself. If the press reported worsening unemployment, the press, rather than unemployment, was the main problem noted by the Reagan administration. Reporting unpleasant news could be regarded as an extremely insensitive act. People would become upset unless the administration knew how to back away from messengers of bad news.

Though it is difficult to judge which of these two explanations better accounts for the public's reaction, each explanation standing alone points to the existence of societal

problems that existed in the United States in the fall of
1983. Why had the media lost the confidence of the American public? Could it be possible that the government's antagonism toward the media had been contagious?

Public indifference to the government's exclusion of the
media was one of the more significant elements of the invasion. There seemed to be collective disinterest in news
apart from what the government provided, although this
disinterest did not include everyone. This fact was especially significant since the invasion occurred at the same
time that U.S. military involvement in Central America was
expanding daily. One might have expected, therefore, demands for a full accounting of the reasons for the invasion.
Instead, even though the administration's main justification—that of "rescuing" American medical students—was
roundly disputed, the invasion aroused little sustained interest.

The government's treatment of the press had few prece-
dents. White House spokesman Larry Speakes said shortly
after the invasion that the White House had "overlooked"
the press in its rushed planning of the mission. Some reporters, however, had heard rumors and when they questioned the White House about an invasion, they were told
that none was in progress. Additionally, Caribbean leaders
knew of the mission at least forty-eight hours before it took
place, making it seem that there was time for consideration
of the media.

The more plausible explanation is that the government's
total blackout of the press was entirely deliberate. Since the
Vietnam War, reporters were regarded as a major liability in
any overseas operation. Before Grenada, the administration had taken many steps to inhibit press coverage on
other issues of foreign policy. In this light, the Grenadian
incident can be seen as the culmination of a multipronged
plan by the government to centralize the flow of information and limit the role of the media.

APPARENT NEW RELATIONS WITH THE FOURTH ESTATE

During its first three years, as has been noted, the Reagan administration tried unceasingly to narrow the role of the media. It used legislative proposals and White House directives to implement permanent change, and it adopted day-to-day operational restrictions to protect various agencies from outside examination. In February 1984 the administration's policy seemed to shift as the White House announced that it would withdraw portions of the March 1983 directive, including the provisions for prior review and the use of lie detectors. Spurred by proposals submitted by major media organizations, Pentagon officials held hearings on the press curbs during the Grenada invasion.

About the same time, Charles Wick, head of the U.S. Information Agency, apologized for having wiretapped numerous conversations without informing participants, in violation of government regulations. The USIA also apologized for maintaining for two years a secret black list of individuals who should not be sent overseas on speaking engagements because they were not sympathetic enough with the administration's policies.

This apparent change in the administration's attitude toward the Fourth Estate received much press attention. Its real meaning, however, was unclear, particularly since the 1984 presidential campaign season had already begun. If the administration was ready for a different relationship with the Fourth Estate, it needed to do more than withdraw temporarily from a few of its many plans to close Washington off from access by the media and other public groups. Damage inflicted by the 1982 Executive Order on Classification needed to be undone, and many other agency rules and procedures for responding to information requests had to be revised.

Chapter 7

INDIRECT CONNECTION
Scientific Inquiry
and National Security

In this so-called information age, scientific inquiry and technological invention have become tools of political power. The health of national economies and superior military capability depend on rapid advances in such areas as electrical engineering and computer system design. The new importance of the results of scientific research has intensified a fundamental controversy between those who would restrict the flow of scientific information in the interest of national security and those who would encourage that flow to ensure American excellence in science and education.

THE ISSUES

Proponents of stricter controls maintain that national security is increasingly dependent on the country's technological superiority. A 1976 report by the Department of Defense concluded that the United States was losing its technological and economic lead by giving adversary nations access to information crucial to the continued strength of the nation. Moreover, it said that there had been numerous instances of other nations' stealing technological secrets. In 1982, the FBI charged eighteen men, including Japanese business executives from Hitachi Ltd., with paying undercover agents several hundred thousand dollars to steal technological data on new IBM computers. A similar incident involving the Chinese government's alleged smuggling of equipment used for radar jamming and electronic surveillance took place the following year.

Since the early 1970's, concern over the appropriation of scientific research by adversary nations has led to efforts by the federal government to tighten controls over sharing such information. This trend grew more pronounced in the 1980's as a result of a deepening conviction on the part of government officials involved in military planning and intelligence that strict limits on the sharing of scientific information were vital to national security.

In opposition to this view, the academic and scientific communities have argued that U.S. superiority can be maintained only in an open environment. Moves to restrict the sharing of unclassified information with researchers from other countries and to attach classification rules to government-funded research will only retard scientific inquiry and will discourage talented people from undertaking government-funded research. Moreover, numerous academics and scientists maintain, in regulating universities, the government has gone after the wrong institutions, since vital secrets are usually obtained through commercial rather than research channels.

The debate concerning secrecy and scientific freedom is often formulated in terms of the need to strike a balance between national security and the traditional emphasis on unrestricted academic and scientific pursuits. This approach is correct, however, only if restrictions on research can be shown actually to prevent unauthorized access to information of vital interest to the nation. This issue further breaks down into two other basic tasks: to define national security in relation to science and to locate the channels of unauthorized transfer of technological information. In the 1980's, while these issues were being vigorously debated, the government markedly increased its efforts to attach secrecy controls to scientific activity.

RESTRICTIVE LAWS AND REGULATIONS

Before Reagan took office, there were already four major laws on the books giving the government control over the results of scientific research. Most of these laws were directed at material goods, not at ideas or information associated with research. The Reagan administration has applied these laws to ideas as well.

The first of these laws, the Inventions and Secrecy Act of 1951, gave defense agencies authority to review patent applications to determine if their publication would be harmful to the national security. In 1981 this law was applied to a voice scrambler invented by three Seattle engineers and, in 1978, to a data-protection device invented by a professor at the University of Wisconsin.

A second law, the Atomic Energy Act of 1954, governs the classification of information related to nuclear weapons and nuclear energy. Information relating to nuclear weapons and nuclear energy is "born classified" under this law—as soon as such information comes into existence it becomes a government secret. According to Mary Cheh, a noted expert on government laws relating to information, government officials have generally applied the born-classified law only to information generated by the government. Yet this policy is changing. According to Cheh, the problem here is that "a scientist in a university laboratory, a researcher in a private plant or an enterprising citizen can all independently compile, develop or invent Restricted Data. Their work is then secret and subject to government suppression." The Atomic Energy Act was used in 1979 to prohibit the publication of an article titled "The H-Bomb: How We Got It, Why We're Telling It" in *The Progressive* magazine. And in December 1981, the Department of Energy attempted to use this law to require the directors of many scientific laboratories to have their employees cease all meetings and correspondence with researchers from the Soviet Union and Eastern bloc countries.

Under the Arms Export Control Act of 1976 and ancillary regulations, the State Department maintains an extensive list of munitions for which an export license is required. The implementing regulations cover unclassified information used in the design, manufacture, and operations of thousands of items, as well as "any technology which advances the state-of-the-art or establishes a new art in an area of significant military applicability in the U.S." According to recent administrations, technical data sent out of the country, Americans going abroad to attend conferences, and information disclosed to foreign visitors to the United States are all considered exports. The Reagan administration has used this law to bar foreigners from conferences and to prevent foreign students from enrolling in physics, computer, and other science courses.

Like the Arms Export Act, the Export Administration Act of 1979 is vast in scope. It authorizes the Commerce Department to place restrictions on the export of technologies that can be used for both civilian and military purposes. This law may be used to prohibit export that might endanger national security, to implement foreign policy, and for other reasons.

In addition to its extension of these four laws, raising the issue of whether laws originally aimed at products should be applied to information, the Reagan administration has actively fostered integration between the academic and industrial sectors. Several of Reagan's science advisers considered the isolation of the academic community from industry to be largely responsible for what they saw as the nation's sluggishness in turning research into new products.

Consequently, although the government in the 1980's continued to increase the budget for research and development, it moved to make research contracts contingent on the scientists' willingness to work on applied rather than basic research. In addition, the government sought more influence over the transfer of sophisticated technologies to foreign countries. Many companies, however, complained that the government's desire to tie exports to politics would inhibit their international operations and allow nations such as Japan and West Germany to move ahead of the United States. Both businessmen and academics have argued that restrictions on their activities should be narrowly defined in order to advance the nation's true security interests.

Still further restricting the freedom of scientists are two orders issued by the Reagan government: the classification order of 1982, previously discussed in chapter 2, which authorized federal officials to classify information, and the directive of March 1983, which required government officials, ex-officials, and contractors with the federal government who had access to classified information to sign prior-review agreements. Both of these significantly expanded government control over the dissemination of scientific papers and put researchers on government-funded research projects in continual jeopardy of violating secrecy limitations.

Finally, there were restrictions issued by more than fifteen government agencies involved in overseeing scientific activities. Particularly diligent in this regard were the departments of Defense, Commerce, and State.

WIDE-RANGING EFFECTS

The necessary conditions for the pursuit of scientific knowledge involve much more than isolated laboratory research. Frank Press, president of the National Academy of Sciences, has stated, "The health of the research enterprise depends crucially on scientists building on each other's ideas and on the ability to test new ideas against the *best* ideas *worldwide*. The informal exchange of draft scientific papers among leading specialists in the field, travel to scientific meetings and conferences, personnel exchanged, and the publication of papers and their exposure to global scrutiny by other researchers . . . are the *essence* of productive science."[1]

Government attempts to limit the free flow of ideas has extended to many areas of the scientific and academic communities. One area is attendance at conferences. On occasion, American scholars who wished to attend foreign conferences in order to present research papers have been required to obtain permission under the Arms Export Act or other regulations. A widely publicized incident occurred in 1980 when several Eastern bloc scientists were prohibited from attending a conference on bubble memory, lasers, and electro-optical systems—technologies with possible military applications.

Universities have been ordered to keep foreign visitors and exchange students under surveillance to ensure they did not gain access to sensitive information. In the 1980's the State Department, which had set up an exchange program with the specific purpose of helping China in high-technology areas, attempted to put pressure on several universities who had accepted students under this program to keep the students away from recent work in computer science. Administrators at the University of Minnesota were told by the State Department that a Chinese student attending the university was to have no access to unpublished or government-funded research or computer hardware. Peter McGrath, president of the university, said that these restrictions "struck at the very heart of a free university, if not of a free society, for they advocated secrecy and surveillance, the restraint of expression and the disregard of academic freedom."[2]

Restrictions were also imposed directly on scientific research and publication. In 1977, the Commerce Department and the State Department warned the organizers of two open scientific meetings that papers scheduled for presentation contained sensitive information that if released would violate export controls. That was one of the first times that scientists became aware that laws governing the export of products were being extended to include the transfer of ideas. Numerous instances of this application followed this incident.

In 1982, five days before a conference on electronic engineering was to open in Philadelphia, government reviewers at the U.S. Air Force Systems Command indicated that three papers on integrated digital circuits, which had already been printed and made available to reporters, could not be published. The conference managers were asked to remove the papers from an already printed Conference Digest and to ask reporters who had received copies to return them. After the conference administrators raised numerous objections, including the fact that the papers covered topics of no particular relevance to military systems, the Air Force reversed itself and allowed the papers to be presented. On other occasions, researchers have been subjected to lengthy interrogation over articles submitted to scientific journals during which unclassified information was reclassified. Editors of the distinguished monthly publication of the Institute of Electrical and Electronics Engineers, *Spectrum,* have received phone calls from military officials ordering them to shred articles "immediately."[3]

The Reagan directive of March 1983, requiring government contractors to submit papers for prepublication review, potentially had far-reaching consequences for individual researchers, since many of those who receive government contracts at some point become privy to highly sensitive material. Under the directive, these people could be subjected to lifetime restrictions on their publications and, in addition, could incur civil penalties for the unauthorized sharing of restricted information.

Equally disconcerting for many researchers was the classification order of 1982. Its terms were anything but clear. Although it retained an earlier rule that basic research should not be classified, it did not indicate how basic and applied research could be differentiated. Moreover, it put the burden of initial decisions whether to share research on the scientists.

In addition, the classification order removed all constraints on the classification of unclassified material. On account of this provision, the results of research contracts could be classified at any time. Even before the order was issued, recipients of federal research grants had become concerned by the fact that results of originally unclassified research were, on occasion, classified on the eve of publication, as almost occurred at the Philadelphia conference described here.

The order also created a new category for the classification of information related to the "vulnerabilities or capabilities of systems, installations, projects or plans relating to the national security." Potentially, scientific theories, computer systems designed for civilian use, and decoder devices fit in this category. Going a step further, in the 1980's, the Air Force and the Department of Defense several times moved to block the presentation of papers containing unclassified information that was only remotely relevant to military systems.

Many university administrators and researchers protested the vagueness of the classification order and the confusion that resulted from so many agencies imposing controls. Such decentralization left much opportunity for controls to be misapplied by those who might not understand or appreciate the nature of scientific inquiry. The crux of the new classification is that government may now exercise control over many projects in which the researcher was previously left alone. Even if the fruits of research in a particular project are never classified, the possibility of government interference is likely to have far-ranging chilling effects.

A FULL-FLEDGED DEBATE

The administration's restrictions on the scientific community gave rise to intensified debate in 1982 when Admiral Bobby Inman warned participants at a scientific symposium that there would be pressure for legislation to stop the "hemorrhage of the nation's technologies" unless scientists agreed to stricter controls in certain areas. He proposed experimental restrictions on commercial hardware and software, cryptography, and other electronic information.

In response to Inman's warning, a panel of experts was appointed by the National Academy of Sciences to examine various aspects of the application of controls to scientific communication and to suggest how to balance the competing objectives of national security and free exchange of ideas. Its task involved a careful assessment of the sources of leakage, the nature of universities and scientific communication, and the costs and benefits of controls. The panel was sponsored by the Department of Defense and prominent scientific organizations and was briefed by intelligence experts. It was chaired by Dale Corson, president emeritus of Cornell University, and included people who had spent years doing government-funded research or holding high-level positions in the Department of Defense, the National Security Agency, and other departments concerned with the topics under review.

After a year, the panel issued a report titled "Scientific Communication and National Security." The report concluded that the transfer of technology related to military purposes was a growing problem but that very little of it had occurred within the scientific and academic community. The government's restrictions were seen to weaken both the military and economic capacities of the country by "restricting the mutually beneficial interaction of scientific investigators, inhibiting the flow of research results into military and civilian technology, and lessening the capacity of universities to train advanced researchers." The panel also denied that there was any serious contest between universities as educational institutions and the national security. Instead, it emphasized the importance of maintaining conditions of research that were attractive to talented people in the fields of engineering and science. The panel recommended that no restrictions of any kind limiting access or communication should be applied to any area of university research, unless it involved a technology that met all of four criteria developed by the panel: the technology (1) was developing rapidly and the time from basic research to application was short; (2) had direct military applications with or without civilian use; (3) would, if transferred, give the Soviet Union a significant near-term advantage; (4) was considered restricted by other countries as well as the United States.[4]

Other studies were conducted during the same period as the National Academy of Sciences investigation. The recommendations from these reports covered the full spectrum from strict government control to very little control apart from areas of military intelligence and equipment. Notably, defense expert Edward Teller and Admiral Inman have urged that any restrictions be narrowly confined to the intelligence community or to clear dangers to the national security.

Increased government control of scientific information may be inevitable until the overall outlook of the government changes. Colin Norman, who has written frequently on this topic for *Science* magazine, believes that such restrictions will continue. He has called this policy a serious "erosion at the edges of scientific communication." In the spring of 1984, the press reported that the presidents of Stanford University, the California Institute of Technology, and the Massachusetts Institute of Technology had jointly protested a new Defense Department proposal that would allow military reviewers to veto the publication of findings on unclassified research that had not previously been subject to restrictions. Marvin Goldberger, president of the California Institute, said that they were reacting to what appeared to be a very disturbing trend. "The essence of our letter was that the types of restrictions being considered could well make it impossible to accept certain contracts. . . . It's the nose of the camel that we are worried about," he said.[5]

The nation's principal scientific organizations have by now formulated positions in opposition to this trend. Stephen Unger, professor of computer science at Columbia University, has called the debate over national security and scientific freedom a pseudo-conflict. In his view, which is shared by many proponents of open scientific inquiry, national security is secured through open communication. That is, the argument in favor of secrecy is fundamentally flawed by a failure to appreciate that the Soviet Union remains behind, not because it does not have access to information, or lacks intelligent scientists, but because of its pervasive secrecy system, which chills all exchanges, even within the Soviet Union.

William D. Carey, chief executive officer of the American Association of the Advancement of Science, has written that "circumstances that make America strong depend on consensus, not coercion. Government controls inject an element of suspicion. As trust recedes can mutuality of interest survive?"[6] This question, perhaps, best captures the essence of the present conflict between certain government agencies and the scientific community, which very clearly must work together to protect the nation's technological and defense capabilities. The issue of control over scientific inquiry is likely to be one of the more significant aspects of government information policy for the remainder of this century.

Chapter 8

DON'T TAKE THOSE NUMBERS AWAY!
Cutbacks in Federal Statistics

STATE GOVERNMENTS NEED INFORMATION, UNIFORMLY PRESENTED, ABOUT OTHER STATES. PRIVATE INDIVIDUALS AND BUSINESSES NEED UNIFORMLY PRESENTED INFORMATION ON A WIDE VARIETY OF ECONOMIC AND DEMOGRAPHIC MATTERS. THE FREE MARKET ECONOMY IS A MARVELOUS MECHANISM, BUT ONE OF THE PRECONDITIONS FOR ITS EFFECTIVENESS IS THE AVAILABILITY OF INFORMATION TO PARTICIPATE.

—Dr. Courteney Slater,
former chief
economist for the
Department of Commerce

An important function of the federal government, affecting each individual, community, and profit-making and nonprofit entity, is the collection and analysis of statistics. Americans live in a quantitative society. We use numerical estimates to chart literacy rates, unemployment, poverty, economic deficits, and the quality of life. Many of these figures are eagerly awaited and are often the subject of political controversy.

The statistical activities of the federal government have grown in both size and complexity in this century. Today, more than ninety different government bodies are concerned with the preparation of data that are used for economic planning, law enforcement, housing programs, environmental policy, and various other purposes. Close to 75 percent of all the domestic expenditures of the federal budget are indexed to statistical formulas. The Department of Commerce formulates the national accounts; the Bureau of Labor Statistics provides information on employment, productivity, and wage levels; the Statistical Reporting Service in the Agriculture Department reports on crop levels and prices; and the Internal Revenue Service provides essential data on income levels. Yet, despite their importance, statistical activities have generally been considered merely the boring handmaiden of more dramatic government programs that are easier to visualize.

In the 1970's, the growing importance of statistics drew attention from both private and government users of federal statistics. Two studies of the problems in the production and organization of federal statistics were conducted, one by the Commission on Federal Paperwork and the other by the President's Reorganization Project for the Federal Statistical System. Both reports recommended substantial strengthening of statistical policy through departmental reorganization and large increases in financial support.[1]

A major concern of these reports was that high-level policymakers did not seem to understand the extraordinary significance of statistical activities. According to James T. Bonnen, an economist and director of the study of statistical programs made for the Carter administration, since the 1960's, statistical programs have been aimed toward short-term political objectives and "all too frequently flit rapidly from one ideological goal, media or market event after another."[2] The number of professional statisticians at the OMB had declined from 69 in 1947 to 29 in 1977 during the period that saw the largest expansion of new statistical programs and data collections in the nation's history.

The Government as a Collector of Statistics

The United States is alone among other developed countries in having no central office to collect statistical data. Instead, this activity is decentralized throughout the government, an arrangement that allows specialization but creates problems of duplication and lack of coordination. Before the 1930's, no agency had authority for relating the work of one statistical agency to another. In 1939, an office was established in the Bureau of the Budget (later the Office of Management and Budget) to promote more efficient statistical operations. Not long after that, the agency was given control over all agency forms for collecting information that involved nine or more people or organizations. During the Carter administration, functions relating to governmentwide coordination of statistics were transferred to the Department of Commerce.

The Reagan administration was committed to shrinking the power of the federal government, including its role of providing objective, reliable data. As part of its policy of deregulation of industry and decentralization of services, it planned to tailor the federal collection of data to the needs and priorities of the federal government and to leave the collection of data for other purposes to the private sector. Collection activities retained by the government were increasingly required to pay for themselves by fees charged to users. Figures formerly required by state and local governments were no longer to be provided. With these plans, which aroused great controversy in the early 1980's, the administration was abandoning the long-standing tradition of the government as the principal source of information about the economic and social conditions of the nation.

The plans were implemented under the Paperwork Reduction Act of 1980, by which Congress relocated statistical policy and coordination functions in a new office in the OMB. According to many who testified in hearings conducted in 1982 and 1983, Congress unwittingly helped destroy the role of the federal government as a collector of reliable and essential statistical information. Since the Paperwork Act did not establish separate goals for statistics, this area was subordinated to the other OMB objectives of cutting the budget and deregulating industry. Pursuant to the Paperwork Act, the OMB began to assemble, on an annual basis, a budget for collecting information. Each year, it set a quantitive limit on the demands that federal agencies could place on the private sector, on state and local governments, and on individuals in collecting federal data. A stringent total reduction of 25 percent was established for the first two years, during which time many statistical programs were eliminated.

Besides statistical policy, the OMB was in charge of the clearance of forms, regulatory policy, privacy regulations, and the introduction of up-to-date telecommunication facilities. According to a 1983 report of the General Accounting Office, this arrangement did not leave the OMB with either the budget or personnel to carry out its responsibilities for statistical coordination and evaluation.[3]

The cutbacks in statistical information carried out in the early 1980's were of long-term significance. Data series need continual fine tuning in order to be of high quality. Gaps in data series and disruptions in the recruitment and training of qualified personnel can take years to reverse. Policy changes are harder to assess without reliable data. At a time when major responsibilities are being transferred to the state and local level, statistical data are more than ever essential for the optimal allocation of block grants used for nutrition, welfare, agricultural research, and education. Unfortunately, as Rep. Jack Brooks of Texas has stated, "Right now, when we desperately need more and better data on the state of this nation's economy and the condition of its people, the very information we need is disappearing."[4]

EFFECT OF BUDGET CUTBACKS ON STATISTICAL OPERATIONS

Although statistical programs comprised only a very small amount of the federal budget, they were substantially affected by the across-the-board budget reductions during the first years of the Reagan administration. Fifty-eight data series were reduced in scope or dropped entirely.[5] Among the programs then eliminated were the Census Bureau's survey on energy consumption, monthly department store sales data, and the annual housing survey. *The Statistical Reporter,* a monthly publication that had served as a useful summary of changes in statistical programs, was eliminated. By way of organizational change, the Statistical Policy Coordinating Committee, an interagency forum for policy development in which all cabinet-level departments and the Council of Economic Advisers, the Federal Reserve Board, and the OMB were represented, was done away with; so also was the separate Statistical Policy Office in the OMB.

There were large staff reductions in the principal agencies. In the first year of the administration, 319 people at the Census Bureau were "riffed"; another 500 were downgraded or reassigned. The National Center for National Education Statistics, the National Center for Health Statistics, the Department of Agriculture's Statistical Reporting Service, and the Energy Information Administration all suffered decreases in the numbers of people assigned to statistical operations. Changes in personnel affected, on the one hand, long-term research and methodological improvements and, on the other, regular programs for quality maintenance. Equally important, the cuts caused many of the most talented people working on statistics to leave their government posts and, according to informed sources, also deterred many younger people from taking positions in government.

ENERGY

Two of the statistical areas most severely affected were energy and health care. At the Energy Information Administration (EIA), longer-term analyses of the supply and demand for oil, natural gas, coal, nuclear energy, electric power, and alternative fuels were eliminated. The administration also ended the Industrial Sector Survey, which provided information on conservation efforts and the impact of fuel prices on industrial costs. According to the OMB, "withdrawal from energy policies based on market intervention has reduced the need for data to design, implement and evaluate such policies."[6] This view, however, overlooked the importance of statistics to monitor the consequences of turning to the forces of the marketplace to guide the deployment of energy resources and disregarded the needs of the private sector and of local governments for data in the aftermath of deregulation. Only after many of its statistical programs were dropped, did the EIA ask the Committee on National Statistics of the National Academy of Sciences to determine the important needs of the public for energy data. This request covered issues that would appropriately have been raised earlier, including the cost and best methods of collection of data about energy resources. This example of preliminary research after the fact was typical of many cutbacks in statistical programs in the administration's early years.

Health Care

Drastic cuts in the area of health-care statistics caused reductions in the scope of surveys conducted by the National Health Interview Survey. The National Health and Nutrition Examination Survey, which had formerly come out every five years, was changed to come out once every ten years; the National Nursing Home Survey from once every three years to once every six years.

The domino effect of such reductions in sample size or changes in periodicity provoked protest from administrators of local programs. Thomas J. Ward, chairman of the Advisory Committee for the Pennsylvania State Health Data Center, wrote the head of the House Subcommittee on Census and Population in 1982 that cutbacks in statistical programs were having an adverse impact on the planning and evaluation of local health programs. He wrote, "When these states must discontinue transmittal of Vital Statistics data to the National Center for Health Statistics, the national data base will no longer be available, since individual states are the sole source of Vital Statistics data. Moreover, the United States would become the only industrialized nation in the world lacking such information, which also provides information on the leading causes of death, life expectancy, infant and maternal mortality and fertility trends."[7]

An official from the Connecticut Department of Health Services, Susan S. Addiss, testified in 1982 that state policymakers and health workers needed federal statistics in order to set program priorities and evaluate the outcomes of specific projects by comparing them with data derived from other states and towns. Delays in the issuance of 1980 Census figures, she said, were hindering important decisions by Connecticut legislators about the allocation of funds to care for the elderly because of the nonavailability of figures concerning the size and location of the elderly population. In addition, the elimination of training programs run by the National Center for Health Statistics for state government personnel who prepared data for the national health data banks was likely to bring about an overall deterioration in the quality and comparability of the data submitted. Addiss' main point was that federal statistical resources were especially needed at a time when more program responsibilities were being transferred from the federal to the state level. "The current and proposed budget reductions in various Federal data-producing programs severely threaten the States' ability to carry out their new responsibilities," she said.[8]

THE CENSUS

Another area where limitations on statistics threatened seriously to undermine programs of vital importance involved the Census Bureau in the Department of Commerce. Data provided by the Census are used extensively by the private sector and government agencies at all levels. The apportionment of electoral representation is based on census data, which are also the basis for virtually all market research information on incomes and other household characteristics.

Over 25 percent of the annual budget of the Bureau of the Census is associated with funding from other agencies. Hence, the large reductions in the budgets of those agencies in fiscal year 1982 diminished research and data processing at the Census Bureau. The overall quality and timeliness of the bureau's reports were endangered, and improvements were canceled or delayed.

Since 1978, funds had been designated for the design of a Survey of Income and Program Participation, which would measure more completely and accurately the effects of the government's antipoverty and welfare programs. According to a Congressional Research Service report, by 1981 more than $20 million had been spent on this project, on which several different agencies had worked. The Reagan administration would have abandoned the survey if Congress had not allocated specific funding for its completion.[9]

As an additional result of cutbacks, the sample size for one of the key elements of the Census data, the Current Population Survey, was reduced by 16 percent. Also, there were long delays in the release of data from the 1980 Census. Figures, including information on population and housing, were not released until 1983. A primary data tape was given to a private company, which sold the information at inflated prices before the government shared census information with the public. On account of the delay, company decisions regarding the location of new stores and the distribution of products were postponed, as were programs managed by local government agencies.

CONSUMER PRICE INDEX AND LABOR STATISTICS

One of the most important statistical series is the Consumer Price Index (CPI). It is the official measure of price change in consumer markets, defined in reference to a fixed market basket of goods and services. Many labor agreements are pegged to it, as are Social Security benefits. About once each decade, the Bureau of Labor Statistics (BLS) revises the CPI to take account of new products and improved methods. Because of budget cutbacks, this update was delayed by several years.

Also at the BLS, budget cuts required the elimination of, or reduction in, data series essential to labor, including

some required in legislation. Wage surveys for several industries were eliminated. The Family Budget Program,
which showed the costs of food and shelter for the working
family and which was used in calculations of university
scholarships, alimony cases, and collective bargaining, was
also done away with. In 1982, economist Markley Roberts
testified on the AFL-CIO's concern about a decline in the
quality and volume of federal data regarding occupational
health and safety as well as in data needed for labor-
management relations. He emphasized that only figures
produced by the government were acceptable to labor and
management as a basis of negotiations. Additionally, federal statistics were needed to monitor international trade
and employment. Roberts estimated that it would take the
Bureau of Labor Statistics ten years to recover from the
reductions that had taken place.[10]

ELIMINATION OF THE STATISTICAL POLICY OFFICE AND REDUCTIONS IN AGENCY STAFFS

The administration's explicit downgrading of statistics as
a priority of federal activities was symbolized by the decision to do away with the separate Statistical Policy Office in
the OMB.

The question whether there should be a central office, or
perhaps a separate agency for statistical policy and coordination, has been debated in government for years. As recently as 1982, the economist Wassily Leontief, speaking to
the Joint Economic Committee of Congress, urged greater
attention to the need for better coordination of federal statistics. He stated: "The United States is the only advanced,
industrialized country that still does not possess a real, central statistical office responsible for collection, systematic
organization and dissemination of facts and figures pertaining to population, natural resources, technology and other

aspects of the national economy and society. Confronted with a giant jigsaw puzzle, economists and statisticians working in the government or private business, as well as those engaged in academic research, spend a large part of their time trying to put its pieces together, that is, to reconcile incompatible figures coming from different sources to fill as well as they can the gaping holes in the total picture."[11] Others maintain that the more decentralized statistical apparatus in the United States is appropriate to the large, complicated, and geographically dispersed programs that these figures support.

Edwin Goldfield, executive director of the Committee on National Statistics at the National Academy of Sciences, has argued that a central statistical office is necessary to provide leadership. This office "could more than pay for itself, by eliminating waste and upgrading quality of statistical information." Furthermore, Goldfield has said that a central office, working with other federal agencies, has a responsibility to serve the lower levels of government.[12]

The OMB preempted this debate by disbanding the Statistical Policy Office. Morever, for sixteen months, the position of chief statistician remained empty, until Congress insisted that it be filled. The risk, if not recklessness, of these moves, was very great. In a short period of time, the combination of budget cuts, imposition of ceilings for collecting information, departmental reorganization, and staff reductions threatened to destroy large elements of the federal data base.

Nonetheless, the OMB responded to demands that personnel and programs be restored by holding firm to its own evaluation of statistical activities. Christopher DeMuth, the administrator in charge, repeatedly defended the fact that statistics had been lumped together with other OMB functions, including paperwork reduction and deregulation. At a meeting of the Washington Statistical Society in 1983, he maintained that statistical matters should compete with all other claims for attention and resources, without separate treatment.

THE GOVERNMENT'S RESPONSIBILITY

The question of the federal government's responsibility to provide statistical information has been paramount in debates on the administration's view that many existing government activities could be carried out by the private sector. The issue is whether a certain valuable commodity—statistical information—is going to be treated as a public good or a private good.

As the United States has become more of an information-based society, disagreements on this issue have become more intense and of greater importance. On the one hand, many people consider federal involvement essential as growing numbers of citizens need more and more information. On the other, the Reagan administration continues to maintain, in line with its philosophy of reducing the role of the federal government, that federal responsibility for providing information, whether in the form of statistics or other publications, should be curtailed.

According to experienced statisticians and to the dozens of people who testified before Congress in the last three years, the gathering of data in a very large number of areas must be carried out at the federal level. Only thus will the needs of the federal government be satisfied and the economy be propelled forward. Courtenay Slater, former chief economist of the Department of Commerce, has said, "Only the federal government can produce statistical series which are uniform and consistent for the nation as a whole and which are of unquestioned honesty and objectivity. The federal government also has a responsibility to produce statistical information for which there is a national need even if there is not a direct federal government need. State governments need information, uniformly presented, about other states. Private individuals and businesses need uniformly presented information on a wide variety of economic and demographic matters. The free market is a marvelous mechanism, but one of the preconditions for its effectiveness is the availability of information to participate."[13]

Other people maintain that most information is much more useful to the government than the Reagan administration recognized. Goldfield and others have recommended that experiments be conducted to determine the extent of the need for current statistical programs, as well as the feasibility and appropriate methods for implementing user fees, when this option is chosen, to assure that small entities and individuals are not unfairly deprived.

Donald Woolley, chief economist of Banker's Trust Co., provided examples of the private sector's need for federally provided statistics in his 1982 testimony before the House Subcommittee on Census and Population.

> We work with almost all of the banking and financial data compiled by the Federal Reserve System and the federal budget data provided by the Office of Management and Budget and the Treasury Department. But we also use regularly the Commerce Department's national income data and its data on retail trade, homebuilding, nonresidential construction activity, manufacturing and trade inventories, business fixed investment, and the U.S. foreign trade and balance of international payments data, much of which is compiled by the Census Bureau. We rely, too, on the population reports and the data on finances of state and local governments published by the Census Bureau, the data on prices, employment conditions, and wage trends issued by the Department of Labor, and the quarterly financial data covering manufacturing corporations published by the Federal Trade Commision.

Woolley's list did not stop there. In conclusion, he said, "Federal statistics are the only aggregate data available for analyzing national economic trends, for determining economic changes within different regions of the country and for making international economic comparisons."[14]

"CRUNCH OR BE CRUNCHED"

The long-term dangers of the elimination of, and reductions in, statistical operations are of the utmost significance. Gaps in federal data banks could undermine hundreds of programs ranging from Social Security to agricultural productivity. The need for accurate federal statistics is especially acute for states that are faced with the challenges of Reagan's new federalism.

According to a recent study, there are now 150 domestic assistance programs in eighteen federal departments employing a variety of statistical factors to allocate funds. Statistics steer the funding process both for allocating program funds and for determining recipient eligibility for program participation.[15] In 1983, the National Governor's Association sponsored a conference entitled, "State Statistical Survival in the 1980's, Crunch or Be Crunched." An important issue at that time was high unemployment and major changes in the labor force. Yet numbers that would direct spending where it was most needed were no longer available.

Other groups have been similarly confronted with the need for federally gathered numbers. As Katherine Wallman, director of the Council of Professional Associations on Federal Statistics, has stated, "Cutbacks in federal statistical programs won't make anyone hungry . . . at least not directly. But the reductions in federal data collection, analysis, and dissemination activities, which are occurring, will have a profound effect on policy formulation, public and private decision making, research, the distribution of benefits, and the allocation of resources."[16] In an impressive show of solidarity and strength, in the 1980's organizations and companies, labor unions, and nonprofit organizations that depended on statistics banded together to urge the preservation of federal statistical operations. The American Association for the Advancement of Science adopted a resolution calling upon the administration and Congress to recognize the central importance of government statistics and to provide for the improvement of data bases vital to all sectors of society. Perhaps for the first time, data had an organized constituency.

Chapter 9

ON THE FRONT LINE
The Library

THE PICTURE I SEE IS NOT ONE THAT
FURTHERS THE USE OF INFORMATION AS A
TOOL OF ECONOMIC AND SOCIAL DE-
VELOPMENT BUT ONE OF EFFORTS TO RE-
STRICT USE. . . . THE POLITICS OF PUBLISH-
ING IN WASHINGTON HAS BEEN DE-
STRUCTIVE OF BOTH THE INFORMATION
INDUSTRY AND THE EFFECTIVE DISTRI-
BUTION OF GOVERNMENT INFORMATION
TION.

—Robert Hayes, Dean of Graduate
School of Library and Information
Sciences, UCLA, presentation at
American Library Association
annual convention, 1983

To the extent that American society has a nationwide infrastructure for the distribution of information, it is housed in tens of thousands of community, private, nonprofit, and government libraries. Taken together, these institutions make the United States perhaps the most information-rich nation in the world.

The federal government has been a principal supplier of information to many libraries in the form of printed publications, data tapes, microfilm, and audiovisual materials. It employs the largest number of librarians and information specialists. Since its origin in 1800, the Library of Congress has developed extensive collections that are virtually universal in scope. While its first responsibility is to Congress, it also extends service to the general public and to smaller libraries throughout the country. In addition, federal depositories, which are located in every state, receive copies of publications, volumes of hearings, and other records of government activity.

Equitable access to government information is one of the primary tenets of the library community. The American Library Association (ALA), the oldest and largest library organization in the world, believes that "A democratic society depends on the federal government ensuring the right of all citizens of access to a comprehensive range of knowledge and a diversity of communications media. There should be free and equal access to data collected, compiled, produced and published in any format by the government of the United States." The Special Libraries Association and other library interests do not insist that information be free, but they also emphasize the need for information produced by the government to be widely accessible.

More and more, the government has been taking a different point of view, rejecting the notion that information should be made available by the government and seeing it more as a commodity to be managed by private entities. Government thus becomes the information provider of the last resort, producing only information that the private sector is unwilling to provide. This policy is consistent with the broader ideological goal of shrinking the operations of the federal government and caters to the information industries, which have been expanding greatly in recent years.

As the economic value of information has increased, private companies have become interested in providing information formerly supplied by the government. In the past, information in the form of books and research or product advertising was sold in the marketplace. Today, however, data processing and other computerized activities sprung from new technologies have made large quantities of information much more profitable.

This new development has prompted government officials to adopt policies aimed at measuring the economic value of information, with less attention paid to concerns about access. Under the direction of the Office of Management and Budget, in the 1980's an exhaustive review of all information activities by federal agencies was undertaken, with the economic value of information being its overriding focus. The stated goals of this review were to reduce unfair competition with the private sector and to apply cost-benefit analysis. The OMB's criteria included no explicit service component.[1]

During this same period, the library community was affected by other policies of the Reagan administration. The presumption in favor of classifying information to remove it from easy access put more material off limits, while the new, broad application of reclassification created much confusion. In addition, agencywide budget cuts had a drastic impact on the information collections in federal departments, which in turn, had a negative effect on libraries around the country. On account of these and other hardships, the library community was compelled to mobilize in order to demand greater consideration of the government's responsibility as a provider of information to many different sectors of society.

FEDERAL CUTBACKS IN LIBRARY STAFF AND PUBLICATIONS

Across-the-board budget cuts in 1982 caused at several agencies the loss of people who were directly involved in collecting and processing information. Additionally, a general lack of appreciation for such individuals was demonstrated by a proposal from the Office of Personnel Management (OPM) to downgrade the qualification standards for federal librarians, library technicians, and technical information specialists. While this proposal was still being debated, five members of Congress urged OPM to withdraw it, stating it "could encourage the employment of less qualified librarians, and thus endanger the entire information network of the federal government."[2]

John Berry, editor-in-chief of *Library Journal,* wrote a stinging satirical editorial in the form of a letter addressed to OPM director Donald Devine. Berry said, "Maybe you think that because we're mostly women you can push us around, but you must know that those days are long past." He then vividly described the tasks performed by federal librarians. "They are the reference librarians who provide vital, current information to Congress. They are the bibliographers, catalogers, and classifiers who labor to be sure that the libraries of the entire nation build access to their collections in an efficient uniform way . . . that helps make our agricultural system the envy of the world, and helps protect the health of our people."[3] Because of such strong opposition, this proposal had not been settled two years after it was made. In the meantime, the assault on government library personnel proceeded through attrition and heavier work loads.

In addition, many printed materials of value to both agency and nongovernmental collections were eliminated. In April of 1981, a moratorium was imposed on the release of all new publications. Around the same time, the head of the Government Printing Office, Danford Sawyer, announced that in order to counter three years of deficits, the GPO would no longer publish anything that was not guaranteed to yield one thousand dollars. These moves were only a small portion of a well-publicized campaign to streamline government printing. By the end of 1983, more than one-quarter of all government publications that existed in 1980 had been eliminated, a total of 3,850.

These publications appear to have been a mixture of items infrequently released, those issued for one time only, and those published on a regular basis. The administration claimed that they were all examples of government waste. On several occasions, officials amused reporters by reciting titles of such now extinct items as "How to Clean your Kitchen Sink." Also dropped, however, were valuable publications, including *Health Resource News,* a monthly that went to hospitals and state agencies; and the *Selected List,* also a monthly, which contained information on government publications likely to be of interest to the general public. According to Sandra Petersen, a librarian and chair of the American Library Association Government Documents Round Table, libraries and government agencies were hard-pressed to do without materials that had been part of their central files. She singled out *Morbidity and Mortality Statistics,* which had been issued by the National Center for Health Statistics.[4]

While thousands were eliminated, other publications were simply not reissued when anticipated, thereby disrupting library inventory. A 1983 review of GPO publications listed as still in existence indicated that seemingly significant items such as the *Handbook of Labor Statistics* had not been reissued since 1980. Still other publications became more expensive. *Infant Care,* which for fifty-eight years was available free of charge, now sold for $4.75. In 1982, the GPO instituted a minimum price of $1.95 for all publications and doubled the price of many items. This enabled it to earn far more than expected, approximately $5 million that year, and thus drew attention to the basis of its pricing criteria. Some agency staff claimed there was no clear procedure for determining if, when, and for how much, a publication would be available. Others suggested that the fate of various items was determined by politics;

"Economic publications stood a better chance of survival than something on energy conservation," said someone working at the Environmental Protection Agency.

Public library budgets were strained by the transfer of the production of printed and computer-based materials to the private sector. This was a time when the volume of information to be stocked by libraries was growing exponentially. Many university, foundation, and other libraries were looking for ways to pool their resources and were compelled to alter the practice of acquiring nearly everything in categories of interest to their clientele. The extra costs added by private-sector production of previously low-cost federal material was yet another hardship, one that affected public and nonprofit libraries more than those in the corporate sector.

When the *Education Directory of Colleges and Universities* was transferred to a private company, the price nearly tripled. Zipcode data from the 1980 Census, which had demographic information used by local governments, organizations, and businesses, became much more expensive after it was discontinued by Census and picked up by a consortium of private companies. Private publication, however, did not always mean a higher price. Interestingly, the report of the commission headed by J. Peter Grace concerning ways the government could save money was sold for $46.00 by GPO and for only $10.00 by Macmillan Publishing Company.[5]

Private-sector production of government material meant a direct loss for the federal depository program, perhaps the nation's outstanding achievement in providing local communities with easy access to government information. The federal depositories receive most government documents. They are under the auspices of the GPO and are located in every state, at public and private institutions whose main obligation as members of the depository program is to provide free access to the general public.

CONTRACTING OUT

A storm of controversy arose when it became known that several federal agencies were arranging to have their information collections run by private firms. In the fall of 1983, the Department of Energy contracted out its library to Informatics General Corporation. The Department of Housing and Urban Development (HUD) contracted with Aspen Systems, an American subsidiary of a Dutch holding company. While there were many different opinions regarding this type of action, the need for careful evaluation of the pros and cons was stressed throughout the library community.

Anne Heanue, assistant director of the ALA's Washington Office, believed that insufficient time had been given to considering erosion in quality that might result from the changes in personnel and the inventory procedures that might be introduced by an outside entity. Heanue also questioned the propriety of putting government information under the control of foreign companies, as occurred in the HUD instance.[6]

David Bender of the Special Libraries Association (SLA) said that not enough emphasis had been put on the service side of the equation. "Putting libraries in the private sector," he said, "might be dollar wise but not service smart. If the company changes, if the agency gets a new classification rule, who is to ensure continuity in the collection?" The SLA recommended to the Office of Management and Budget, which was in charge of procurement, that the government retain responsibility for long-term, core federal information and that task-oriented work be handled by contractors. It also recommended the addition of several requirements to the OMB's procurement procedure, including a study of the number of displaced workers and a survey of national library resources to allow a comprehensive assessment of the results of transferring different government collections and projects to the private sector.

In conversation, Bender indicated that the SLA, a largely private-sector organization, certainly was not opposed to the idea of contracting out but was concerned about the maintenance of "a collective memory" through the development of procurement methods that appropriately weighted the social value of government-held information.[7] Yet both Congress and the executive branch may be headed in the opposite direction. New OMB criteria for contracting out say nothing about low-cost access and other noneconomic factors that might favor the government retaining control. The libraries of small agencies are allowed to bypass entirely the procurement procedures established in the new policy.

THE COLLECTIVE MEMORY

The central issue in the contracting out debate seems to be, to use Bender's phrase, what types of information presently collected and stored by the government are part of the nation's collective memory and should continue to be made available by the government. In the late 1970's, a task force was appointed by the National Commission on Libraries and Information Science (NCLIS) to study the relationship of private-sector and government information activities. It came to the conclusion that "at the very least, there is information that government must provide—a record of its actions, explanations of the law, descriptions of services." Members of the task force were split regarding how much of the remaining activities should be transferred to the private sector.[8] The position of the ALA and certain other library organizations is that "a democratic government has an obligation to make available to all citizens the results of its actions, including its information collecting activities and its research and development efforts."[9] The ALA believes this information should be widely available regardless of a person's ability to pay and that the government has an affirmative role to play in demonstrating the value of information as a societal resource.

In this debate, the Reagan administration emerges as a true radical, ready to reverse long-standing principles of equitable access. Its guiding principle appeared to be the OMB's policy guideline that "information is not a free good but a resource of substantial economic value and should be treated as such." The emphasis here on economic value can sidestep important constitutional issues pertaining to the needs of an informed electorate or on people's need for various types of government information in order to protect themselves and their loved ones from environmental pollutants and other hazardous conditions.

DISCRIMINATORY ACCESS

On account of higher prices for government publications and other policies of the Reagan administration, public access to information became more dependent on one's level of income. This applied to individuals, libraries, small businesses, and local government.

In 1982, another NCLIS task force studied the impact of user fees and other trends on cultural minorities. As reported in *Library Journal,* the task force concluded that "Funds should be made avilable to prevent barriers which are the result of insufficient numbers of staff, cost of automated services which cultural minorities are unable to afford." It also recommended that user fees be avoided for materials of importance to the general population.[10]

The seriousness of the price issue arises in connection with new technologies for processing and packaging information. Should they be included in the price for government information? Do public groups have the same right of access to machine-readable data files as they do to printed material? Both the ALA and the Private Sector/Public Sector Task Force of the NCLIS have taken the position that the costs of creating or collecting information should be borne by the government. Prices should only reflect the true cost of access and reproduction. Eileen Cooke, ALA director, has stated that other fees will surely create divisions between the information-haves and have-nots, the latter including those for whom the cost of necessary information has been priced beyond their means.

On occasion, as happened with the 1980 Census, the administration has made information available to the private sector on an exclusive basis or long before it was released to other groups. Additionally, agencies are increasingly putting information in data banks and charging for retrieval. According to Matthew Lesko, author of *Information USA,* today the great majority of government information is not in the channels most familiar to the general public, such as the GPO and the Consumer Information Center. Will technology and government-industry pacts relating to more sophisticated forms of information stand in the way of the tradition of equitable access? There is a clear need for national policy regarding these items on the emerging new agenda regarding access to information.

Chapter 10

CONCLUSION
The Mosaic of Government Secrecy

In the final quarter of the twentieth century, information confers power as never before. Those who own and control information have great advantages over those who do not, ranging from profits to political power. In these circumstances, the government's handling of information serves to unify the population or, on the contrary, drives different sectors even further apart. In recent years, excessive emphasis on ideology and ill-considered actions that have significantly reduced the federal government's role as an information provider have erected serious obstacles to public communication and have tainted society's most valuable resource: public information. As Floyd Abrams, a prominent First Amendment attorney, wrote in the fall of 1983, the administration "acts as if information were in the nature of a potentially disabling disease which must be feared, controlled and ultimately quarantined."

Since uncontrolled information was believed to bring about evil consequences, the Reagan administration restricted the entry of foreign publications, films, novelists, and distinguished political figures. Experienced and loyal people who have served in the United States government were told they must sign nondisclosure agreements that would oblige them for the indefinite future to seek official approval prior to sharing their valuable political ideas and analyses. Such restrictions drive talented, patriotic people away from government service and breed apathy and fear.

On numerous occasions, the administration justified its secrecy regulation on the grounds that the public would not know how to make proper use of the information received from a wide variety of sources. This attitude throws into question the very foundation of a society based upon people's electing representatives after a careful weighing of competing information and ideas. The implicit message of those who would restrict access to the speeches of a Gabriel Garcia Marquez or Ian Paisley or the plays of Italy's brilliant political playright Dario Fo, is that only those in power are capable of deciding wisely and, therefore, should exercise absolute control.

The politics of secrecy began long ago. It is an intricate mosaic of tangibles and intangibles carried out directly through laws, lies, and misinformation and indirectly through insider habits that shield those in office from public scrutiny. It is a practice that serves specialized interests both inside and outside government. Yet, despite its complexity, secrecy sanctioned by the upper reaches of government and extending beyond can have but one possible result: an increasingly arrogant government and an uninformed citizenry.

The main issue addressed here is not whether the Reagan government was more sinister than other administrations but, rather, how, wearing ideological blinders, it has successfully instituted permanent threats to constitutional liberties that in less arrogant administrations would very likely have been softened by criticism and debate. The information restrictions of the Reagan government are of historic value: they will outlast his administration or reappear in amended form in the future, unless appropriate measures are taken to prevent this from happening.

Efforts to comprehend the significance of government secrecy measures and cutbacks in the provision of information should examine closely their purported objectives. Under Reagan these included deregulation, efficiency in government, and national security. Such words and phrases often obscure the actual impact and intention of government information policies.

For example, deregulation has been embraced in various sectors without being understood. Specifically with regard to information, deregulation may bring about the absence of critically important data about such issues as food and drug safety, environmental pollution, and employment. Debate concerning the government's responsibility to make this kind of information widely accessible began before the current administration and will continue in the future. The nexus between deregulation and public—as well as government—knowledge merits further examination.

The objective of efficiency in government, also, is a complicated matter. Eliminating publications that are superfluous may be efficient; eliminating materials whose lack necessitates employing experts to provide the missing information would be inefficient. Furthermore, important decisions that will significantly affect the flow of public information are rarely justifiable on the grounds of efficiency alone. Social benefits and constitutional liberties are the broader context for narrow considerations of efficiency.

The federal government today has ultra-sophisticated tools for efficiently intervening in people's lives, even as it refuses to provide information about its own activities. In 1984, the administration moved to link itself by computer with the bigger national credit agencies. Previously, it had expanded the use of computer matching which, according to OMB, could efficiently save government much money and time by comparisons that "involve names, social security numbers, addresses, government contract numbers, numbers on bills or invoices, etc."

The third objective of the Reagan restrictions involves national security. What, by the way, is the national security? When was this phrase last defined in any way that limited its application? Surely, this catchall phrase has been used carelessly by every president, with diminishing effectiveness until we are now at the point where punishments for violating national security-based regulations must be disproportionately severe in order for them to be taken seriously. Reagan found it necessary to impose criminal sanctions and lie detector tests to get the point across that he had declared war on leaks, for example. This severity perhaps was clear evidence that he and others had overused national security as a rationale for their actions.

If this policy continues, the ground rules of the American political system will change dramatically. Sweeping threats and classification rules will have undermined all hopes of open government and participatory decision making. This is the situation that Orwell captured so well in his novel *Nineteen Eighty-four,* where the Party's control over historical and political information and its incessant control over people's thinking eliminated the very possibility of political thought. As the principal character, Brian Winston, realizes at one point: "Freedom is the freedom to say that two plus two makes four." If that is granted, all else follows.

Today a major obstacle to a citizen's ability to say two plus two equals four is the prevalence of official misinformation. A continuous menu of half-truths weakens the ability to reason effectively. The sheer volume of misinformation in the public forums today regarding significant issues is, in itself, a serious obstacle to popular participation.

In his own charming television appearances, President Reagan excelled as a master of misinformation. Elizabeth Drew, writing about Reagan's 1984 State of the Union Address, captured this ability in her comment that "The most striking thing about the President's speech, beyond its politics, was its pyrotechnical display of Reagan's rhetorical devices and skills. It's not simply the husky voice speaking practicedly into the microphone—making a much greater impression on the viewer at home, at whom it is aimed, than on the people in the House chamber, who are props. It's more Reagan's unique use of language and his patented uplift tone."

But what happens to political debate in the course of this performance? Drew continues, "Reagan throws around questionable numbers to a degree that may be unprecedented. He dazzles with his statistics, and he grins and glides away from problems with more agility than any other President in history. Reagan understands the importance of having a vision and stating it forcefully. . . . People who intrude with facts are 'doomsayers' and 'handwringers' who must be ignored."

Reagan's success, of course, says much about the direct conflict between sanitized packaging of political information and serious efforts to address difficult subjects. Reality fades as a speaker who is in a position to speak authoritatively instead tells saccharine tales about his own childhood that somehow are relevant. The basic problem with this approach is that it spreads a false view of a very complicated reality, meaning that problems will not be addressed until they are greatly aggravated. The requirement that truth remain attractive means that anyone with complaints or problems should be ignored. "Just pretend it's not there" is not a satisfactory political message today, nor was it ever.

Additionally, such an approach breeds intolerance and suspicion. Those aberrant souls who dare to exercise their constitutional rights in a hostile environment are described as society's enemies and even as terrorists.

The search for ways to reverse recent restrictions on public access to information can begin now. The initial task is to study these changes, a difficult project since the flow of information is redirected silently and, for the most part, without public notice. Moreover, some of the most important areas to be investigated are quite intricate. For example, the budget contains many hidden agendas that bear upon access to information. Yet even David Stockman confessed to William Greider in 1982, "None of us really understands what's going on with all these numbers." Similarly, to perceive the implications of the reorganization of the executive branch and the extraordinary increase in the authority of the Office of Management and Budget requires the skills of a detective.

Some remedies, however, could be instituted in the near future. Congress could enact a permanent moratorium on implementation of the presidential directive that imposes lie detector tests and prepublication review for all federal employees with access to classified information. It could amend the McCarran-Walter Act to prevent its use to exclude foreign visitors who pose no threat, and it could also provide standards for the disclosure of information. Legislative action is needed to set standards for classification and, importantly, to temper the all-out movement to eliminate paperwork with procedures that guarantee that necessary data will be retained.

Additionally, congressional policies in the areas of privacy, intelligence gathering, and the application of advanced information technologies merit public attention. So do current efforts to impose political conditions on scientific research and university instruction. The wide scope of the work to be done is a reason to begin now, building on the actions of many individuals and organizations that are already engaged in monitoring the government's handling of information. The greatest obstacle to government secrecy has always been the dynamic, pluralistic nature of American society. Common ground can be sought on the terrain of government information policies.

Chapter 11

PRYING OPEN THE LID
Directory of Public Organizations

Veteran defenders of the First Amendment such as the American Library Association and the American Civil Liberties Union have been joined by a growing number of organizations that devote all or a significant part of their resources to monitoring the information policies of the federal government. Several new groups have emerged in direct response to what they perceive as the ignorance or indifference of Washington officials regarding the federal government's responsibility to provide essential information. For example, public- and private-sector interests that became concerned about the cutbacks and absence of quality control in federal statistical programs formed a new organization in 1980 called the Council of Professional Associations on Federal Statistics. OMB Watch, a small, energetic group that tracks and educates the public about the vast increase in the power of the Office of Management and Budget, was established in 1983.

More than a dozen groups are monitoring government restrictions on the sharing of scientific information, and at least that many take an active role monitoring congressional and executive branch activities with regard to the Freedom of Information Act. In each area of social regulation, including health care, environmental safety, and communications, there are community and public organizations that have opposed the recent dramatic change in the information gathering and dissemination functions of federal agencies. Such groups, taken together, comprise a valuable network of expertise about government information activities, including privacy law, classification, and the use of new technologies to process and store information. Moreover, these groups are helping to elevate the federal government's handling of information to the level of a major national policy concern, which is where it belongs.

The next several pages provide a selected list of organizations that can furnish additional information about the topics covered in this book. Presented according to chapter headings, names, locations, and brief descriptions are given for groups that have special expertise in different areas. These are only some of the many organizations nationwide that have committed themselves to the furtherance of open government and responsible federal information programs.

THE WHITE HOUSE, GENERAL

The American Civil Liberties Union
132 West 43rd Street
New York, NY 10043
(212) 944-9800

Washington Office/ACLU
600 Pennsylvania Avenue, S.E.
Washington, D.C. 20003
(202) 544-1681

The ACLU is a nationwide organization dedicated to defending civil rights and liberties under the U.S. Constitution. It acts to protect public freedoms in legislative, judicial, and administrative forums.

PUBLICATIONS (selected): *ACLU Lawyer*
Free Speech 1984, The Rise of Government Controls on Information, Debate and Association

Common Cause
2030 M Street, N.W.
Washington, D.C. 20036
(202) 833-1200

Common Cause is a nonprofit, nonpartisan citizen's lobby. It monitors activities of the Reagan administration regarding the FOIA and is generally concerned about the issue of openness in government. In this respect, it has sought to insure that government hearings are open to the press and the public.

PUBLICATION: *Common Cause,* magazine published in six bimonthly issues a year

Fund for Open Information and Accountability, Inc.
339 Lafayette Street
New York, NY 10012
(212) 477-3188

The Fund was formed to defend, enforce, and strengthen the right of the public to know what the government is doing and to hold it accountable, by assisting groups and individuals to obtain and interpret government files through the FOIA; by publicizing the existence, uses, and importance of the FOIA and its relationship to other vital issues; and by building and working with networks and coalitions of groups and individuals interested in obtaining information under the FOIA.

National Coalition Against Censorship
132 West 43rd Street
New York, NY 10036
(212) 944-9899

The Coalition promotes and defends First Amendment values of free thought, inquiry, and expression; encourages, supports, and coordinates activities of national organizations in opposition to censorship; opposes restraints on open communication; and supports access to information.

PUBLICATIONS: *Censorship News,* a quarterly newsletter, and occasional reports on pertinent topics

People for the American Way
1424 16th Street, N.W., Suite 601
Washington, D.C. 20036
(202) 462-4777

This nonprofit, nonpartisan organization is dedicated to protecting First Amendment rights and freedoms. Areas of specialization include contemporary issues regarding the separation of church and state and book banning.

PUBLICATIONS: *Quarterly Report,* a newsletter
Protecting the Freedom to Learn, a citizen's guide to intellectual freedom

Privacy Journal
P.O. Box 15300
Washington, D.C. 20003
(202) 547-2865

The Journal informs individuals about their rights to privacy and to have access to their medical, government, school, credit, employment, and insurance records. It monitors societal trends, such as the rights of privacy of individuals who subscribe to two-way cable television and individual rights in light of the increasing use of polygraph tests and computer matching.

PUBLICATIONS: *Privacy Journal,* an eight-page magazine published monthly
"Are You Now or Have You Ever Been in FBI Files?"

OFFICE OF MANAGEMENT AND BUDGET

OMB Watch
1201 16th Street, N.W., #405
Washington, D.C. 20036
(202) 822-7860

OMB Watch monitors the activities of the OMB in connection with the budget and federal regulatory policies.

PUBLICATION: *OMB Watch,* a newsletter

REGULATORY AGENCIES

Alliance for Justice
600 New Jersey Ave., N.W.
Washington, D.C. 20001
(202) 624-8390

The Alliance is an association of organizations concerned with protecting the environment, consumer interests, and the rights of minorities and women.

PUBLICATIONS: *Undermining Public Protections: The Reagan Administration Regulatory Program* (1981)
Contempt for Law: Excluding the Public from the Rulemaking Process (1983)

American Federation of Labor and Congress of Industrial Organizations (AFL/CIO)

815 16th Street, N.W.
Washington, D.C. 20006
(202) 637-5000

The AFL/CIO monitors federal policies concerning worker health and safety, including OSHA regulatory programs.

Children's Defense Fund

1520 New Hampshire Avenue, N.W.
Washington, D.C. 20036
(202) 483-1470

The Fund monitors federal policies that affect the health and welfare of children. It participates in related congressional and administrative proceedings.

Natural Resources Defense Council

1725 I Street, N.W.
Washington, D.C. 20006
(202) 223-8210

The Council pursues legal activities to protect global environmental integrity. Its areas of interest have included the Campaign to Save EPA, the Clear Air and Clean Water projects, energy conservation, public health, and nuclear nonproliferation.

PUBLICATIONS: *The Synfuels Manual*
Hitting Home—The Effects of Reagan's Environmental Policies on Communities Across the Country
The Amicus Journal, a quarterly publication

Office of Communication
United Church of Christ
105 Madison Avenue
New York, NY 10016
(212) 683-5656

The Office of Communication is the instrumentality of the United Church of Christ that works to further public interests in relation to the mass media. For twenty years, it has played an active role in administrative, legislative, and judicial proceedings that bear upon the goals of equity and diversity in communications.

PUBLICATION: *Parties in Interest: A Citizen's Guide to Improving Television and Radio*

Public Citizen
2000 P Street, N.W.
Washington, D.C., 20036
(202) 293-9142

Public Citizen has launched an Open Government Project, an ongoing study of the governmental agencies and their change of information policy under the Reagan administration. It is examining the areas of statistics, consumer publications, labeling of consumer products, and research budgets.

PUBLICATION: *Public Citizen,* a quarterly magazine

Public Citizen Health Research Group
2000 P Street, N.W.
Washington, D.C. 20036
(202) 872-0320

This nonprofit, consumer-advocacy organization monitors drug safety, medical device safety, and occupational health and safety issues pending before the FDA and OSHA. It publishes reports and provides testimony at government hearings.

PUBLICATION: A free publication list of the group's many titles is available.

Sierra Club
330 Pennsylvania Avenue, S.E.
Washington, D.C. 20003
(202) 547-1141

The Sierra Club is devoted to the study and protection of the earth's scenic and ecological resources. It focuses its attention in the areas of public lands, pollution issues, and energy.

PUBLICATION: A listing of Sierra Club books is available.

United Mine Workers Union
900 15th Street, N.W.
Washington, D.C. 20005
(202) 842-7200

This union pursues more effective OSHA regulations and enforcement in the area of health and safety for mine workers.

CONGRESS

The American Jewish Congress
15 East 84th Street
New York, NY 10028
(212) 878-4500

The Congress works to advance civil rights, protect civil liberties, defend religious freedom, and safeguard the separation of church and state. It submitted comments on the Reagan classification order to Congress and has closely tracked the administration's actions relating to the First Amendment.

Campaign for Political Rights
201 Massachusetts Ave., N.E.
Washington,D.C. 20002
(202) 547-4705

The Campaign monitors U.S. intelligence agencies at home and abroad. It defends the rights of individuals to speak and organize and advocates increased access to government information.

PUBLICATION: *Organizing Notes,* a newsletter

Center for National Security Studies
122 Maryland Ave., N.E.
Washington, D.C. 20002
(202) 544-5380

The Center houses the American Civil Liberties Union (ACLU) project on National Security claims that bear upon individual freedoms. It examines the policies of the government—particularly the executive branch—focusing on individual rights pertaining to the First, Fourth, and Fifth Amendments.

PUBLICATIONS: *Litigation Under the Federal Freedom of Information Act and the Privacy Act,* a manual edited yearly, currently in its eighth printing
Using the Freedom of Information Act: A Step-by-Step Guide

THE MEDIA

American Newspaper Publishers Association

Newspaper Center
Box 17401
Dulles International Airport
Washington, D.C. 20041
(202) 620-9500

The Association is a trade organization of some 1,400 member newspapers from the United States and other nations in the western hemisphere. It is an active proponent of effective enforcement of the FOIA.

American Society of Newspaper Editors

P.O. Box 17004
Washington, D.C. 20041
Contact: Richard M. Schmidt, Jr., ASNE's legal counsel
Cohn and Marks
1333 New Hampshire Ave.—Suite 600
Washington, D.C. 20036
(202) 293-3860

The Society has a membership of more than 900 editors of daily newspapers in the United States and Canada. Its principal purpose is to serve as a medium for the exchange of ideas and the professional development of its members. For several years the Society's Freedom of Information Committee has campaigned against secrecy in the government.

PUBLICATION: *The Bulletin,* a magazine published nine times a year

Freedom of Information Center

School of Journalism
P.O. Box 858
University of Missouri at Columbia
Columbia, MO 65205

The Center is a clearinghouse that monitors governmental, societal, economic, and legal controls on information. Its concerns include matters of censorship, First Amendment rights, and freedom of information.

PUBLICATIONS: *Freedom of Information Center Report;* published 18 times a year, provides detailed discussions of First Amendment issues, the FOIA, and other government activities related to communications
FOI Digest, a bimonthly newsletter

National Federation of Press Women, Inc.

Box 99
Blue Springs, MA 64015
(816) 229-1666

The objectives of the Federation are to advance the standards of journalism and to provide a forum for the exchange of ideas and experiences of working professionals in communications. It takes an active role in First Amendment and freedom of information issues through congressional testimony, publications, and educational programs.

National Freedom of Information Committee

Gannett News Service
P.O. Box 7858
Washington, D.C. 20044

The main focus of the Committee is to monitor press freedom and issues concerning the First Amendment as they come before Congress and the courts.

PUBLICATIONS: An annual report, which includes stories of national interest concerning the press and the First Amendment
Periodic press releases and occasional *FOI Alert* bulletins

National Newspaper Association
1627 K Street, N.W., Suite 400
Washington, D.C. 20006
(202) 466-7200

The Association represents 5,000 weekly and 700 daily newspapers across the country. It works to make community publishers' interests known and protected within the federal government and judiciary. The NNA's staff works on a variety of press issues, including those of freedom of information, privacy, and access to information.

PUBLICATION: *News Media Update,* a biweekly newsletter published in conjunction with the Reporters' Committee for Freedom of the Press

Reporters' Committee for Freedom of the Press
800 18th Street, N.W., Suite 300
Washington, D.C. 20006
(202) 466-6313

This legal defense and research organization is dedicated to the protection of the First Amendment rights of the media.

PUBLICATIONS: *News Media and the Law,* a quarterly magazine
News Media Update, a newsletter published twice monthly in cooperation with the National Newspaper Association

The Society of Professional Journalists, Sigma Delta Chi
840 N. Lakeshore Dr., Suite 801 W.
Chicago, IL 60611
(312) 649-0224

This organization is dedicated to the establishment of professional journalism standards and to keeping journalists abreast of legislative and judicial developments in the field.

PUBLICATION: *The Quill,* a monthly magazine

COMMITTEE FOR SCIENTIFIC FREEDOM AND RESPONSIBILITY

American Association for the Advancement of Science
1515 Massachusetts Avenue, N.W.
Washington, D.C. 20005
(202) 467-5238

The AAAS monitors government policy that bears upon the work of scientists at home and abroad.

American Association of University Professors
1012 14th Street, N.W., Suite 500
Washington, D.C. 20005
(202) 737-5900

The Association's interest is the development and implementation of standards concerning academic freedom and tenure. The AAUP is the representative chapter for collective bargaining and government regulations pertaining to any legislation and policy affecting higher education.

PUBLICATION:　*Academe,* a journal published six times a year

Organization of American Historians
112 N. Bryan Street
Bloomington, IN 47401
(812) 335-7311

The Organization is concerned with issues of censure and document disclosure. Access to documentation is a primary interest. Towards this end, it has been a plaintiff in suits restricting access to government documents.

PUBLICATION:　*The Journal of American History,* a quarterly
　　　　　　　magazine

FEDERAL STATISTICS

Council of Professional Associations on Federal Statistics
806 15th Street, N.W., Suite 440
Washington, D.C. 20005
(202) 783-5808

The Council is interested in monitoring and improving the integrity, quality, and accessibility of federal statistics. Its primary focus is on the 10 major statistics-producing agencies of the federal government.

PUBLICATIONS:　*News from COPAFS,* a monthly newsletter
　　　　　　　A list of references on federal statistics and statistical policy is available; it contains subcommittee hearing records and several other items, which are definitive works.

LIBRARIES

American Library Association
50 E. Huron Street
Chicago, IL 60611
(312) 944-6780

Washington Office
110 Maryland Avenue, NE
Washington, D.C. 20002
(202) 547-4440

The ALA is the oldest and largest national library association in the world. Throughout its history it has taken an active interst in the information activities of the federal government.

PUBLICATIONS: *American Libraries,* a journal published monthly
Two excellent chronologies of Reagan information restrictions
Legislative reports of the ALA Washington Office (semi-annual)

Special Libraries Association
235 Park Avenue South
New York, NY 10003
(212) 477-9250

The SLA is a professional association of 12,000 librarians, information managers, and brokers of information. It advocates government policies that retain some responsibilities for the collection and dissemination of information about the economic and social activities of society and its citizenry.

PUBLICATIONS: *Special Library,* a monthly magazine
SpeciaList, a monthly newsletter

NOTES

Chapter 1

1. "Some Atomic Tests Being Kept by the Administration," *New York Times,* 29 January 1984.
2. Department of Energy, proposed rule 10 CFR, Part 1017, "Identification and Protection of Unclassified Nuclear Information," *Federal Register,* 1 April 1983, 13988 ff.
3. Office of Management and Budget, Circular A-122, proposed January 1983, amended 3 November 1983.
4. Emanuel S. Savas, *Privatizing the Public Sector: How to Shrink Government* (Chatham, N.J.: Chatham House Publishers, 1982), 34.
5. House Committee on Post Office and Civil Service, Subcommittee on Census and Population, *Impact of Budget Cuts on Federal Statistical Programs,* Hearings, testimony by Donald E. Woolley, Serial No. 97-41, 16 March 1982, 43.

Chapter 2

1. House Committee on Government Operations, *Security Classification Policy and Executive Order 12356,* Report, 12 August 1982.
2. Richard M. Neustadt to Glenn English, chairman, House Subcommittee on Government Information and Individual Rights, 5 May 1982.
3. House Committee on Government Operations, *Security Classification Policy and Executive Order 12356,*3.

159

4. Freedom of Information Act, 5. U.S. Code, sec. 552 et seq. as amended.

5. "Executive Order 12356 on National Security Information," 47 *Federal Register* 14874, 2 April 1982, effective 1 August 1982.

6. Floyd Abrams, "The New Effort to Control Information," *New York Times Magazine,* 25 September 1983.

7. *National Security Decision Directive 84,* 11 March 1983.

8. More information about Project Democracy became available during 1983 as congressional hearings were held on the administration's proposal.

On March 10 the *Christian Science Monitor* reported that the proposal included a $15 million grant to the Asia Foundation; a $1 million grant to assist Liberia's transition to democracy; approximately $11 million to support Centers for Democracy abroad; $5.5 million to make American textbooks available overseas; $1 million to support a regional newspaper for the peoples of Honduras, Guatemala, and El Salvador; and additional funding to host symposia aimed at building positive attitudes toward democracy.

In October 1983 at a presidential press conference, Reagan answered a reporter's question about the purpose of Project Democracy by saying: "What we have in mind is that the Marxist-Leninists and the world Socialist movement, for that matter, have been ardent missionaries for their beliefs. . . . The proposal is for people to go and be the same kind of missionaries and see if they cannot explain democracy [19 October, 1983]."

Congress has established a private-sector institute for democracy, comprised of corporate and labor representatives, to plan conferences and regional centers overseas. An interagency committee, including the State Department, the U.S. Information Agency, and the International Broadcasting Commission, has been established to carry out other parts of the project.

9. Paperwork Reduction Act of 1980, 44 U.S. Code, sec. 3501 et seq.

10. "Executive Order 12291 on Federal Regulation," 46 *Federal Register* 13193, 17 February 1981.

11. *Reform 88,* Press Clips, distributed by White House Press Office, September 1982.

Chapter 3

1. "Executive Order 12291," 46 *Federal Register* 13193, 17 February 1981.
2. William Greider, *The Education of David Stockman* (New York: E. P. Dutton, 1981), 19.
3. Presidential Task Force on Regulatory Relief, *Reagan Administration Regulatory Achievements,* Report, 11 August 1983, 79.
4. State of the Union Message, 25 January 1984.
5. Office of Management and Budget, *Information Collection Budget of the U.S. Government/Fiscal Year 1984,* 1984, 3.
6. James T. Bonnen et al., "Improving the Federal Statistical System: Report of the President's Reorganization Project for the Federal Statistical System," *Statistical Reporter* 80–82 (May 1980): 197–212; Joseph W. Duncan and William C. Shelton, *Revolution in United States Government Statistics, 1926–1976* (Washington, D.C.: Department of Commerce, Office of Federal Statistical Policy and Standards, 1978).
7. Senate Committee on Governmental Affairs, Subcommittee on Information Management and Regulatory Affairs, Hearings, 6 May 1983, 60.
8. Ibid., 99.
9. General Accounting Office, *Implementing the Paperwork Reduction Act: Some Progress but Many Problems Remain,* Report of the comptroller general, 20 April 1983.
10. Ralph Nader, "Don't Let the Sunshine In," *The Nation,* 7 November 1981, 470.
11. Congressional Research Service, *Presidential Control of Agency Rulemaking: An Analysis of Constitutional Issues that May Be Raised by Executive Order 12291,* 15 June 1981.
12. Susan J. Tolchin and Martin Tolchin, *Dismantling America: The Rush to Deregulate* (Boston: Houghton Mifflin, 1983).
13. Interview, 26 August 1983.
14. The quotes in this paragraph are from the House Committee

on Government Operations, Subcommittee on Legislation and National Security, Hearings on Office of Management and Budget's proposed Circular A-122, 10 November 1983.

Chapter 4

1. Clean Air Act, 42 U.S. Code, sec. 103.
2. Office of Management and Budget, *Paperwork and Red Tape: A Report to the President and Congress,* 1978, 11.
3. Ibid., 22.
4. "Executive Order 12044, Improving Government Regulations," *Federal Register,* 23 March 1978.
5. Interview, 6 November 1983.
6. Interview, 4 November 1983.
7. Alliance for Justice, *Contempt for Law: Excluding the Public from the Rulemaking Process,* Monograph (Washington, D.C.: Alliance for Justice, 1983).
8. Interview, 20 January 1984.
9. Interview, 20 January 1984.
10. House Committee on Government Affairs, Hearing on regulatory reform, testimony by Eula Bingham, 16 June 1983.
11. Congressional Research Service, Environment and Natural Resources Policy Division, *Current Status of EPA Regulatory Agenda Originally Published on 14 January 1981,* Report to the House Committee on Government Operations, 29 September 1981.
12. House Committee on the Judiciary, Subcommittee on Administrative Law and Government Relations, Hearing on H.R. 2327, testimony by Frances Dubroski, 29 June 1983.

Chapter 5

1. "Executive Order 12356 on National Security Information," 47 *Federal Register* 14874, 12 April 1982, effective 1 August 1982.
2. House Committee on Government Operations, Subcommittee on Government Information and Individual Rights, *Free-*

dom of Information Act Oversight, testimony by Bob Schieffer, 14, 15, 16 July 1981.

3. Interview, 26 January 1984.
4. Department of Energy, proposed rule 10 CFR, Part 1017, "Identification and Protection of Unclassified Nuclear Information," *Federal Register* 13988, 1 April 1983.
5. Department of Energy, Hearing on proposed rule 10 CFR, statement by Sandra K. Petersen, 16 August 1983; aforementioned quotes from Stanford University and Hugh DeWitt, comments submitted to the DOE hearing.
6. Sixteen House members to the secretary of the Department of Energy, 24 May 1983. Several senators also publicly opposed the DOE's proposed regulation.
7. Intelligence Identities Protection Act of 1982, Public Law 97–200, 23 July 1982.
8. Senate Committee on the Judiciary, Subcommittee on Security and Terrorism, Hearing, statement of the Reporters Committee for Freedom of the Press by Jack C. Landau, Clemens P. Work, and Deborah J. Lesser, June 1981.
9. House Committee on Energy and Commerce, *Contempt of Congress: Congressional Proceedings Against James Watt for Withholding Subpoenaed Documents and Failure to Answer Questions,* Report, 3 September 1982.
10. Ibid., 38, 39.
11. Interview, 24 January 1984.
12. Interview, 24 January 1984.
13. *United States* v. *Nixon,* 418 U.S. 683,706 (1974).
14. House Committee on Energy and Commerce, Hearing, 28 September 1983.
15. House Committee on Energy and Commerce, Subcommittee on Telecommunications, Consumer Protection, and Finance, *Broadcast Regulation: Quantifying the Public Interest Standard,* Hearing, 24 May 1983, 39–40.

Chapter 6

1. Excellent chronologies can be obtained from the Reporters Committee for Freedom of the Press and the Center for Na-

tional Security Studies, both organizations based in Washington, D.C.

2. For a light-handed treatment of Reagan's errors see Mark Green and Gail MacColl, *There He Goes Again: Ronald Reagan's Reign of Error* (New York: Pantheon Books, 1983).

3. House Committee on Government Operations, *Executive Order on Classification, 12356,* Hearings, 10 March, 5 May 1982, 90–94.

4. "Executive Order 12356 on National Security Information," 47 *Federal Register* 14874, 2 April 1982, effective 1 August 1982.

5. These new categories were for information regarding "vulnerabilities, or capabilities of systems, installations, projects or plans relating to the national security" and "confidential sources."

6. "Executive Order 12333 on United States Intelligence Activities," 46 *Federal Register* 59941, 4 December 1981.

7. Jonathan C. Rose, assistant attorney general, Memorandum to agencies, subject: FOIA Fee Waivers, 7 January 1983.

8. Editorial, *Wall Street Journal,* 5 January 1984.

9. House Committee on Government Operations, Subcommittee on Government Information, Justice, and Agriculture, *Oversight of the Federal Privacy Act and Related Problems,* Hearing, statement by Jack C. Landau, executive director of Reporters Committee for Freedom of the Press, 8 June 1983.

10. William French Smith, attorney general, "Guidelines on Domestic Security/Terrorist Investigations," 7 March 1983.

11. In the Pentagon's *Preliminary Report* on Grenada, 16 December 1983, the primary reason for the invasion was said to be ensuring the safety of American lives.

12. Editorial, *Time,* 7 November 1983.

13. Several television commentators, including John Chancellor and David Brinkley, testified in Congress on the Grenada episode.

Chapter 7

1. House Committee on the Judiciary, Subcommittee on Courts, Civil Liberties and the Administration of Justice, *1984: Civil*

Liberties and the National Security State, Hearings, testimony by Frank Press, 3 November 1983.

2. House Committee on the Judiciary, *1984,* Hearings.
3. House Committee on the Judiciary, *1984,* Hearings. Testimony by Karl F. Willenbrock, chairman of the Technology Transfer Committee of the IEEE, recounts the two incidents described here.
4. National Academy of Sciences, Committee on Science Engineering and Public Policy, *Scientific Communication and National Security,* Report by the Panel on Scientific Communication and National Security (Washington, D.C.: NAS, 1982).
5. "Three Major Research Centers Reject Censorship," *New York Times,* 10 April 1984.
6. William D. Carey, "The Secrecy Syndrome," *Bulletin of Atomic Scientists,* August/September 1983.

Chapter 8

1. "Report of the President's Reorganization Project for the Federal Statistical System," *Statistical Reporter* 80–82 (May, 1980); Commission on Federal Paperwork, *A Report of the Commission on Federal Paperwork: Statistics.*
2. House Committee on Post Office and Civil Service, Subcommittee on Census and Population, *Impact of Budget Cuts on Federal Statistical Programs,* Hearing I, testimony of James T. Bonnen, 16 March 1982.
3. General Accounting Office, *Implementing the Paperwork Reduction Act: Some Progress but Many Problems Remain,* Report of the comptroller general, 20 April 1983.
4. Statement in press release on occasion of release of report of the Congressional Research Service, *Recent Changes in the Coordinating of Federal Statistical Data Collection,* 8 April 1982.
5. Wallman, Katherine Kersten, "Federal Statistics: The Effect of Program Cuts on Availability, Utility and Quality," *Data Use* 10 (December 1982); John H. Aiken, *A Special Report on the Crisis Facing the Federal Statistical System,* Federal Statistics Users' Conference, 12 May 1982.
6. Office Management and Budget, *Principal Federal Statistical*

Programs/Special Report on Statistics Related to the Budget of the United States Government Fiscal Year 1984, 1984.

7. House Committee on Post Office and Civil Service, *Impact of Budget Cuts,* Hearing I, 228.

8. Ibid., 129; Congressional Research Service, *Recent Changes,* 290–304.

9. Congressional Research Service, *Recent Changes.*

10. House Committee on Post Office and Civil Service, *Impact of Budget Cuts,* Hearing I, 51.

11. Joint Economic Committee of Congress, Hearing, testimony by Wassily Leontief, reported by Henry S. Reuss in Hearing I, 157.

12. Interview, 1 October 1983.

13. "Report of the President's Reorganization Project for the Federal Statistical System."

14. House Committee on Post Office anad Civil Service, *Impact of Budget Cuts,* Hearing I, 43.

15. Department of Commerce, Office of Federal Statistical Policy and Standards, *Distributing Federal Funds: The Use of Statistical Data,* by D. Emery, V. Campbell, and S. Friedman, 1980.

16. Wallman, "Federal Statistics," 1.

Chapter 9

1. "Development of an OMB Policy Circular on Federal Information Management," 48 *Federal Register* 40964, 12 September 1983.

2. Rep. William Ford (D-MI), chair of the House Post Office and Civil Service Committee, and four other congressmen to Office of Personnel Management, 12 August 1983.

3. John Berry, "An Open Letter to Donald Devine," *Library Journal,* 15 February 1983.

4. Interview, 2 February 1984.

5. J. Peter Grace, *A War on Waste,* Report of the Private Sector Survey on Cost Control (New York: Macmillan, 1984).

6. Interview, 21 October 1983.

7. Interview, 7 February 1984.

8. National Commission on Libraries and Information Science, *Public Sector/Private Sector Interaction in Providing Information Services,* Report from the Public Sector/Private Sector Task Force, February 1982, xii.

9. Excerpt from American Library Association document in letter from Eileen D. Cooke, director of ALA Washington Office, to Office of Management and Budget, 10 November 1984.

10. *Report of NCLIS on Library and Information Services to Cultural Minorities,* described in "NCLIS and Fees," *Library Journal,* 15 November 1983.

BIBLIOGRAPHY

Abrams, Floyd. "The New Effort to Control Information." *New York Times Magazine,* 25 September 1983.

Alliance for Justice. *Contempt for Law: Excluding the Public from the Rulemaking Process.* Monograph. Washington, D.C.: Alliance for Justice, 1983.

Alliance for Justice. *Undermining Public Protections: The Reagan Administration Regulatory Program.* Prepared by Charles E. Ludlam. Washington, D.C.: Alliance for Justice, 1983.

American Civil Liberties Union. *Civil Liberties in Reagan's America: A Special Two-Year Report on the ACLU's Defense of the Bill of Rights Against Attacks of the Administration and Its Allies.* New York: American Civil Liberties Union, 1982.

American Civil Liberties Union. *Free Speech, 1984: The Rise of Government Controls on Information, Debate and Association.* Report. New York: American Civil Liberties Union, 1983.

Bell, Carolyn S. "The Erosion of Federal Statistics." *Challenge,* March–April 1983.

Berman, Larry. *The Office of Management and Budget and the Presidency, 1921–1979.* Princeton: Princeton University Press, 1979.

Brownstein, Ronald, and Nina Easton. *Reagan's Ruling Class.* Washington, D.C.: Presidential Accountability Group, 1982.

Claybrook, Joan, et al. *Reagan on the Road: The Crash of the U.S. Auto Safety Program.* Monograph. Washington, D.C.: Public Citizen, 1982.

Dorsen, Norman, and Stephen Gillers, eds. *None of Your Business: Government Secrecy in America.* New York: Viking Press, 1974.

Douglas, William A. "Helping Democracy Abroad: A U.S. Program." *Freedom at Issue* (Freedom House), September–October 1982.

Drew, Elizabeth. "A Political Journal." *The New Yorker,* 20 February 1984, 116.

Galnoor, Itzhak, ed. *Government Secrecy in Democracies.* New York: Harper and Row, 1977.

Gottlieb, Daniel, "Notice to Federal Publication Users: Supply Is Down and Prices Are Up." *National Journal,* 6 August 1983, 1634.

Green, Mark, and Gail MacColl. *There He Goes Again: Ronald Reagan's Reign of Error.* New York: Pantheon Books, 1983.

Greider, William. *The Education of David Stockman and Other Americans.* New York: E. P. Dutton, 1981.

Heatherly, Charles, ed. *Mandate for Leadership.* Washington, D.C.: Heritage Foundation, 1982.

Horton, Forest W. *Understanding U.S. Information Policy: The Infrastructure Handbook,* 4 vols. Washington, D.C.: Information Industry Association, 1982.

Lewis, Anthony. "The Right to Scrutinize Government: Toward a First Amendment Theory of Accountability." *University of Miami Law Review* 34 (July 1980): 793–806.

Lewy, Guenther. "Can Democracy Keep Secrets?" *Policy Review* (Heritage Foundation), no. 26 (Fall 1983): 17.

Middleton, Drew. "Barring Reporters from the Battlefield." *New York Times Magazine,* 5 February 1984.

Morgan, Richard. *Domestic Intelligence: Monitoring Dissent in America.* Austin: University of Texas, 1980.

Nader, Ralph. "Don't Let the Sunshine In." *The Nation,* 7 November 1981, 470.

National Academy of Sciences, National Academy of Engineering. *Scientific Communication and National Security.* A report prepared by the Panel on Scientific Communication and National Security. Washington, D.C.: National Academy of Sciences, 1982.

National Commission on Libraries and Information Science. *Public Sector/Private Sector Interaction in Providing Information Services.* Report. Washington, D.C.: National Commission on Libraries and Information Science, 1982.

National Technical Information Service. *Improving Government Resources Management: A Status Report.* Washington, D.C.: National Technical Information Service, 1983.

O'Reilly, James T. "Who's on First: The Role of the Office of Management and Budget in Federal Information Policy." *Journal of Legislation,* Winter 1983, 95–118.

Orwell, George. *Nineteen Eighty-four.* New York: Harcourt, Brace, 1949.

Palmer, John L., and Isabel V. Sawhill, eds. *The Reagan Experiment.* Washington, D.C.: The Urban Institute, 1982.

Peterzell, Jay, "The Government Shuts Up: The Reagan Administration's Stonewalling Reporters." *Columbia Journalism Review,* July–August 1982, 31.

Preston, William, Jr., and Ellen Ray. "Disinformation and Mass Deception: Democracy as a Cover Story." *Covert Action Information Bulletin,* no. 19 (Spring–Summer 1983): 3.

Preston, William, Jr. *Executive Overkill: Secrecy as an Arms Race.* New York: Fund for Open Information and Accountability, 1982.

Relyea, Harold C., et al. *The Presidency and Information Policy.* New York: Center for the Study of the Presidency, 1981.

Rosenbaum, Robert, A., Morton J. Tenzer, Stephen H. Unger, William van Alstyne, and Jonathan Knight. "Academic Freedom and the Classified Information System." *Science,* 21 January 1981, 257.

Savas, Emanuel S. *Privatizing the Public Sector.* Chatham, N.J.: Chatham House Publications, 1982.

Schiller, Anita R., and Herbert Schiller. "Who Can Own What America Knows?" *The Nation,* 17 April 1982, 461.

Schuman, Pat G. "Information Justice: A Review of the NCLIS Task Force Report: Public/Private Sector Interaction in Providing Information Services." *Library Journal,* 1 June 1982.

Simon, Philip. *Reagan in the Workplace: Unraveling the Health and Safety Net.* Monograph. Washington, D.C.: Center for the Study of Responsive Law, 1983.

Sweet, William. "America's Information Effort Abroad." *Congressional Research Reports* 11 (11 September 1981).

Tolchin, Susan J., and Martin Tolchin. *Dismantling America: The Rush to Deregulate.* Boston: Houghton Mifflin, 1983.

Unger, Stephen. "The Growing Threat of Government Secrecy." *Technology Review,* February–March, 1982.

U.S. Congress. House. Committee on Energy and Congress. Subcommittee on Telecommunications, Consumer Protection and Finance. *Broadcast Regulation: Quantifying the Public Interest Standard.* Hearing. 98th Cong., 1st sess. May 24, 1983.

U.S. Congress. House. Committee on Energy and Commerce. *Contempt of Congress: Proceedings Against Interior Secretary James G. Watt.* Report. 97th Cong., 2d sess. September 30, 1983.

U.S. Congress. House. Committee on Energy and Commerce. *Presidential Control of Agency Rulemaking.* Report. 1981.

U.S. Congress. House. Committee on Government Operations. *A Citizen's Guide on How to Use the Freedom of Information Act and the Privacy Act in Requesting Government Documents.* Thirteenth Report. 98th Cong., 1st sess. November 2, 1977.

U.S. Congress. House. Committee on Government Operations. *Administration Proposal Threatens First Amendment Rights of Government Grantees and Contractors.* Hearing. 98th Cong., 1st sess. May 4, 1983.

U.S. Congress. House. Committee on Government Operations. *Executive Order on Security Classification.* Hearings. 97th Cong., 2d sess. March 10 and May 5, 1982.

U.S. Congress. House. Committee on Government Operations. *Federal Statistics and Statistical Policy.* Hearing. 97th Cong. 2d sess. June 3, 1982.

U.S. Congress. House. Committee on Government Operations. *Freedom of Information Act Oversight.* Hearings. 97th Cong., 1st sess. July 14, 15 and 16, 1981.

U.S. Congress. House. Committee on Government Operations. *Reorganization and Budget Cutbacks May Jeopardize the Future of the Nation's Statistical System.* Thirty-fourth Report. 97th Cong., 2d sess. September 30, 1982.

U.S. Congress. House. Committee on Government Operations. *Government Provision of Information Services in Competition with the Private Sector.* Hearing. 97th Cong., 2d sess., February 25, 1982.

U.S. Congress. House. Committee on Government Operations.

Security Classification Policy and Executive Order 12356. Report. 97th Cong., 2d sess. August 12, 1982.

U.S. Congress. House. Committee on Government Operations. *Who Cares About Privacy? Oversight of the Privacy Act of 1974 by the Office of Management and Budget and Congress.* Eighth Report. 98th Cong., 1st sess. November 1, 1983.

U.S. Congress. House. Committee on Interior and Insular Affairs. *Briefing by the Secretary of the Interior.* Hearing. 98th Cong., 1st sess. January 26, 1983.

U.S. Congress. House. Committee on Post Office and Civil Service. *Impact of Budget Cuts on Federal Statistical Programs.* Hearing. 97th Cong., 2d sess. March 16, 1983.

U.S. Congress. Senate. Committee on Governmental Affairs. *Implementation of the Paperwork Act of 1980.* Hearing. 97th Cong., 2d sess. April 14, 1982.

U.S. Congress. Senate. Committee on Governmental Affairs. *Oversight of the Paperwork Reduction Act of 1980.* Hearing. 98th Cong., 1st sess. May 6, 1983.

U.S. Congress. Office of Technology Assessment. *Scientific Validity of Polygraph Testing, A Technical Memorandum.* Washington, D.C.: USGPO, 1983.

U.S. Congressional Research Service. *Recent Changes in the Federal Statistical Programs: An Overview of the President's Budget for FY 83 and Analysis of the Departments of Energy, Labor, and the Bureau of the Census.* Prepared by Daniel Melnick et al. Washington, D.C.: U.S. Library of Congress, 1982.

U.S. Congressional Research Service. *Legal Analysis of OMB Circular A-122, Lobbying by Non-Profit Grantees of the Federal Government.* Prepared by Jack H. Maskell. Washington: D.C.: U.S. Library of Congress, 1983.

U.S. General Accounting Office. *Improved Quality, Adequate Resources and Consistent Oversight Needed If Regulatory Analysis Is to Help Control Costs of Regulation.* Report of the Chairman, Committee on Governmental Affairs, U.S. Senate. November 2, 1982.

U.S. Office of Management and Budget. *Information Collection Budget of the United States Government Fiscal Year 1984.* Washington, D.C.: USGPO, 1983.

U.S. Office of Management and Budget. *Paperwork and Red Tape: New Perspectives, New Directions. A Report to the President and the Congress.* Washington, D.C.: USGPO, 1978.

U.S. Office of Management and Budget. *Principal Federal Statistical Programs: Special Report on Statistics Related to the Budget of the United States, Fiscal Year 1984.* Washington, D.C.: USGPO, 1983.

Wallach, Evan J. "Executive Powers of Prior Restraint of National Security Information: The UK and the USA Compared." *International and Comparative Law Quarterly* 32 (April 1982).

Wallman, Katherine K. "Federal Statistics: The Effect of Program Cuts on Availability, Utility and Quality." *Review of Public Data Use* 10 (December 1982).

Wolfe, Sidney M. M. D., and Barbara E. Freese. "Decreased Law Enforcement at OSHA: FY 1982." Report. Washington, D.C.: Public Citizen, 1982.

INDEX